Animal Farm II - The Machine

Animal Farm II - The Machine

The Self Authoring of Animalkind

Crystal-Dawn

Copyright © 2022 by Crystal-Dawn.

Library of Congress Control Number: 2022914488
ISBN: Hardcover   978-1-6698-2917-1
        Softcover   978-1-6698-2916-4
        eBook   978-1-6698-2915-7

All rights reserved. No part of this book may be reproduced or transmitted in any form or by any means, electronic or mechanical, including photocopying, recording, or by any information storage and retrieval system, without permission in writing from the copyright owner.

Any people depicted in stock imagery provided by Getty Images are models, and such images are being used for illustrative purposes only.
Certain stock imagery © Getty Images.

Print information available on the last page.

Rev. date: 08/05/2022

To order additional copies of this book, contact:
Xlibris
844-714-8691
www.Xlibris.com
Orders@Xlibris.com
843585

Unrestrained Energy

If my embodiment I desired to change, for a new life perspective be gained. I'd choose one of great thoughts, so many a physical form could not contain.

I'd float freely, physical restraints unchained. No needs would have I, just thoughts, materializing thoughts.

And how would such power not be in vain?

I'd divide my focus amongst my three little girls, a hush of sweet whispers their minds I would fill.

Surround them with kindness, faith, love, and goodwill.

And if there's enough of me still, I'd radiate joy through the masses untilled. Just a spark a flame can ignite, a burning so strong it captures the night.

(Crystal-Dawn)

George Orwell once sat with paper and pondered, "How could you communicate with the future?" It was of its nature impossible. He succeeded in achieving the impossible. His literary works will be alive and available to help guide mankind to the brightest future possible.

Crystal-Dawn stared at the screen. She had been planning for years to finish writing her grandfather's stories. Would she be able to capture just the right words to do what needed to be done? Constantly drawn in cross-examination, she shook off the thought. *Focus*, she told herself, *you have the outline, and know the story. Just start writing.*

May 1, 2022

> I am just a poor boy though my story's seldom told.
>
> I have squandered my resistance
> For a pocketful of mumbles such are promises
> All lies and jest
> Still a man hears what he wants to hear
> And disregards the rest, hmm
> (Simon & Garfunkle, "The Boxer")

Crystal-Dawn stared at the screen blankly again. One more cigarette to help clear her mind. She had originally intended to sit and write a simple book, *Animal Farm Part II*. Recently, upon greater research of Grandpa George, she came across his writings of *1984*. Within two days, she had devoured the first eight chapters. The book *1984* was truly a personal message written to the future to avoid the pitfalls of mankind's natural selfish tendencies.

Crystal was amazed by the accuracy of predictions and amused when Grandpa George was off. Of course, there were reasons he couldn't have been too plainly spoken for this book was publicly circulated. Anyone had access to its pages. In 1984, Crystal was conceived. She was born when Rashneesh ended and the spirit of love and community faded from Osho's lifeless eyes. Through the Aquarian lens, she arrived on January 26, 1985, in the mystery cusp. She had a passion for EVERYTHING. Like Boris Pasternak's *Dr. Zhivago*, she loved LIFE.

As Grandpa George had predicted, hope lay with the proles. Whether it was intended to be so, Grandpa met a woman named Constance White in England. A young, wealthy aristocrat from Canada, she had traveled with her two sisters Edith and Mary. Their father was Walter

Woodworth White, a surgeon that served in the legislative assembly of New Brunswick as a member of the conservative party representing Saint John City from 1931 to 1935. He was even the lead surgeon in the Halifax Explosion. They were not in want. It is unknown how Connie, as she was called, happened to carry George's seed, but she carried it all the way back to Canada. A girl was born. Helena. The only child of Constance and her husband John, Helena was sent to boarding schools receiving no love from her socialite parents for not having been born a boy. Growing into an attractive young slender woman, she looked the part of a socialite but was a wild child at heart. She met a German soldier and fell madly in love. His name was Erich Kleinode. He had been a boy of sixteen when the SS soldiers came to his home and took him and his two older brothers. He said in retrospect, "If you are ever asked by your country if you can shoot a gun, say no." His family lived on a sugar beet farm and hunted their own food. They unfortunately had been good with a gun and were sent to the front lines. His short military career as a child was astounding! Current party laws in 2022 make it illegal to tell such stories, and one would most certainly be branded as a racist or worse yet, a Neo-Nazi! The most disgusting feared opponent of all that is good in 2022.

    He tended Adolph Hitler's horses. He said he really liked him at first, but he went crazy. Erich also was on a tank detail where they would sneak in the grass and lay traps. They found a tank, disabled the track, covered the sights with mud, wait for men to open the top, and drop a grenade in. He sat on the top having a cigarette when it blew, killing all inside. We can't be proud of him and the things he did as a child of sixteen. While it was impressive, he never died. The acts he performed were forced upon him as a child. and he rarely spoke of it himself. They lost the war and became the pinup for hatred. Erich was just a smart kid with two older brothers. They were on the front lines of a battle, and he told his brothers to keep their heads down. They didn't listen and as such, each received a bullet to the head. Erich panicked and jumped into the river before them. He was captured by the French. He said they were the most hospitable people, and when they released prisoners at the end of WWII, he made his way to Canada.

Helena and Erich owned a butcher shop in Spiritwood, Saskatchewan. He was a self-taught carpenter that both designed and built many houses, singlehandedly, and with the assistance of his son. Their daughter, Crystal's mother, worked with Helena in the butcher shop. Although Helena was more than willing to walk away from wealth for life as a prole, she had a yearning in her soul that was quenched when she was called upon by Jehovah's Witnesses. There was a time when she would take the *Awake* and *Watchtower* and race to the garbage to see if she could dispose of them before they left the walkway. For some reason, a change occurred in her that made her receptive to the Truth. The Truth is a highly in-depth, perceived cult that started in 1872, and in 2022 it has 8.7 million members. It is in our time the most known and unknown religion that exists to date. They want to tell everybody, and nobody wants to hear. In the purpose of creating the book, *Animal Farm Part II—the Machine*, the Jehovah's Witnesses will be represented by chickens, Henny Penny's if you will. They're found globally and can constantly be heard making sounds. No one actually knows what they're saying, and even if they did listen, it ends in DOOM.

As just predicted, the relationship between Erich and Helena ended in doom. Their daughter was taken to be raised in the Truth. Strangely enough how everything is connected. It was in 1948 that the Shell Lake Massacre occurred. Its sting was felt throughout Canada as the worst family killing at that time. She and her brother went to school with the sole survivor of that massacre. They personally experienced her energy, and both made a point of passing the story to their offspring.

Crystal-Dawn sprung from thought. There were always so many thoughts to be had, so many other thoughts to be considered. One cannot merely exist in a state of thought for there is much doing to be done. The year 2022 was divided into doers and non-doers. The non-doers were typically takers. Not always, as there were always known variances in all species. No one actually spoke of this clear definition of doers and takers. Takers were the ones at the top. The perceived capitalists with top hats, the Mollie Joneses that dreamed of a life of ease. My god, if Grandpa George could have really known this as the future, it is no wonder he pondered, "Why should one feel it to be intolerable unless one had some kind of ancestral memory that things had once been different?"

So many great thinkers and artists have filled the world with all the words and goodness that would be required to start the self-authoring of mankind. Crystal-Dawn knew what needed to be done, at what is considered middle age of thirty-seven to proles, she didn't know if she even had the time required to do what needed to be done. She had been taught from birth that she did not know the hour when her master would arrive but to be at the ready. God would end this system of things, and a new system would begin. The sky was filled with myriads of angels. One clear throne shone in the sky, and the rest of the space filled with the blurred faces of an army, withholding their fury like a ferocious pit bull awaiting its owner's command. Crystal blinked it away. She was outside, sitting on her porch, and her family drove away. It is believed they were going to visit family, help with chores, and visit the cliffs. It must be frustrating for them to have to repeat themselves so many times. Alas, Crystal-Dawn had a full life, and those with full lives do not typically have time to think for themselves.

Human relationships made life harder in 2022, and many had completely given up on them. Crystal believed we truly grow when we interact with as many people as possible. She spoke to anyone that would carry on a conversation, and just as Jesus is a gentleman and does not force himself on others, so too Crystal did not force herself on others. It was more of a playful, heeeey. he had met her life betterer, Gerrasimos during the great Covid. That in itself was a great feat as the party made illegal the visitation of individuals from different households. Like the Brady Bunch, they raised six children together, so conversation was typically drawn to the petty issues typical to paroles. As the mother of the household, and with Crystal's skills excelling at communication in both written and oral and a high capability to use emotion and logic simultaneously, it was her responsibility to be her family's soundboard.

It is difficult to listen. One must put aside their natural inclination to make mental connections to relate to the speaker. You see if the listener is to hear without bias, there cannot be preconceived ideas. This is why George told us, "Until they become consciousness, they will never rebel, and until after they have rebelled, they cannot become consciousness."

Hope Was with the Proles

"Orthodoxy means not thinking—not needing to think. Orthodoxy is unconsciousness."

In 2022, people did not want to think for themselves. The music drowned out the few centimeters of space that was their own. Whether it was music to inspire growth and thoughts or TikTok sounds of nom, nom, nom.

It had been a long time since a musical artist rang out globally to inspire change as Tracy Chapman, John Lennon, and Simon and Garfunkle had once done. Jerusalema soared and inspired many and will join the list of contributing authors to the self-authoring of mankind. World change would take everyone. Not one individual human was the enemy but a brother and a sister in this world we live in and create daily with our actions.

Ahhh, frustration pulsed, making the pressure stronger in Crystal's head. These days, her head almost constantly rang with a pressure pain behind the ears, probably needing more water. We always need more water. The pondering of why we would choose something harmful for ourselves or not intake that which is proven good is just bewildering. In 2022, half of the world does not have a clean water supply while the other half is literally burning fossil fuels, contaminating the water, to recreationally enjoy moving fast over its surface on boats. As a society, they have the technological means to move fast on the water without contaminating it, but the proles striving to join the party will not rise up against their employers and threaten their lifestyle. There are doers and takers throughout all mankind. They are not limited to a race or the user of a substance or a financial bracket. The vast majority of the party was made up of previous proles who had worked hard for their position. Some had indebted themselves financially to join the party. Some gave of themselves sexually. Women were still fighting for equal rights and a true voice. The problem was only that the most extreme voices rang out. A young girl named Gretta fought for immediate environmental protection action. She was discredited for her age, lack of wisdom and her harshness turned the ears of capitalist, conservative Republicans. PETA staged extreme displays to create fear, anger, and disgust. They said they wanted animal rights, which most people do but used hate to fuel the machine to create a bitter decades long battle separating hunters and vegans.

The year 2022 was so full of divisions, and it was only worsening. People of our day NEEDED an "Animal Farm Part II" to see how we have the power to save this planet, ourselves as humans, and all the other species we cohabitate this planet with. Only then when we join together in LOVE for this common purpose, and put all the divisions aside, will we be able to see an end to this system of things and bring about the new system.

Crystal-Dawn went outside again for another smoke break. It was there outside in the open sky that she could see the vastness of the heavens and the great might of God's army. She sat on the paint-peeled porch boards. Her partner repeatedly offered to make her a chair, but she preferred sitting on the ground. The decorative bench that did sit on the porch held a rather large wood elephant. Crystal loved to sit with the elephant in the room and watch people walking by, offering a smile or wave to anyone that would engage. She lived in a natural art studio in Vernon, British Columbia, near the city's main shopping mall. She had held this shop previously as a taxidermy studio but had recently decided against being like ole George Reeves stuck in a superman role. She had a long way to go in her career, and someday her fame would make it clear that she had to be a superman. Taxidermy was just an educational means to an end. Her partner and life betterer Gerrasimos was absolutely everything that Crystal was not and vice versa. It was an amazing partnership made better with loving communication. Nobody is perfect and that is the point. We all carry little pieces of experience to help build each other so we can grow. Gerrasimos is an amazing man and will appear many times throughout this tale as he is truly one of the selfless authors of self-authoring mankind. He deserves his own chapter, no, book. This is not that.

Crystal-Dawn Set Down 1984, Part I Completed

Research is essential to any good writing. Imagine how much research it would take to help mankind learn from their mistakes and realize control is not an illusion, for you have control over the greatest thing in your power—yourself. We can't control others, but without hope and belief that you can trust your fellow man and actually love them with all their beautiful flaws, what future does that leave? It is no wonder suicide rates are so high. Our society goes against nature.

Part I review on current times leaves me completely baffled how George knew this future would come. In my most humble opinion, it proves with enough thought and study of the past, that how it affected the present to create our future is a prediction of possibility. Notes to use for the cross-reference of current 2022 society to *Animal Farm Part II—the Machine*.

1. P. 17 Media

    Wow! Completely flabbergasted! Grandpa George predicted drones! It was not only drones but their use of amazing filming possibilities like that of watching people blown to pieces, like the war in Ukraine right now. Or hatred for Immigrants, that was clear. People most certainly do laugh at others' expense even still. The extremists like it in their pornography, animal fighting, gambling, and secret clubs. The stream is somewhat filtered down to the proles such as *America's Funniest Home Videos* or violent video games and movies. Almost everyone needs their fix though. Hate is recognized as necessary in human emotion, but is violence also? The proles still weed themselves out from violent crimes and shut their ears to their neighbor's screams for help.

    In my personal experience in Kelowna, British Columbia, a woman was murdered in her trailer at a trailer park, not the nice privately owned parks. This park was owned by a large corporation, WestCorp. Not one neighbor called the police. Her blood trail led from one end to the other down the long skinny corridor of the single-wide trailer. It was apparent she had been trapped in the small bathroom for some time as well, viciously getting stabbed over and over.

In the morning the police showed up when Aimee didn't show up for work. They ran their police tape and neighbors pulled couches in the yard to watch the spectacle.

That's all it ever is, a spectacle. It was something to watch and amuse one's self before the police scatter the onlookers. Tracy Chapman spoke of this same occurrence in America. The words resonate through my mind.

Last night I heard the screaming
Loud voices behind the wall
Another sleepless night for me
It won't do no good to call
The police always come late
If they come at all.
(Tracy Chapman, "Behind the Wall")

P. 23 Hatred for Pretty People

He hated her because she was young and pretty and sexless because he wanted to go to bed with her and would never do so.

Many people can relate to wanting someone very badly. The law of repulsion suggests the more you try the more likely you are to not succeed. Taoism suggests being patient and waiting. A good farmer knows fields don't magically sprout food. You need to plant seeds. And even then the weeds still keep popping up. Regardless of our method of pursuing that which we want, how often do we consider that individual's reality?

Only the highly desirable can truly relate to what it feels like going through life having won the biological lottery. Rather than try to relate, most people stoop to jealousy and hatred.

It's shameful for a book to be hated before the reader has read the book thoroughly. Surely a cover could not represent all that is held within?

The beautiful, physically unattainable shall be represented as wolves in *Animal Farm Part II*. "Widely misinterpreted, sometimes feared for their ferociousness, loved for their beauty and loving kindness with each other. They care not for lower species on the food chain and have no problem sustaining themselves off any lower and sometimes higher species.

Remember there are always variables, and wolves, too, fall victim to mankind for the beauty and warmth they offer. Whether allowed to roam free or tied in specialty pens, they are a controlled species.

P. 24 Rhythmic Self-Hypnosis, Chanting

If you missed the previous reference to a TikToc sound, nom, nom, nom, let me enlighten you! The juveniles especially of 2022 are entranced with distracting apps that turn the world's ultimate learning tool into a photo gallery of cute animals, sexy selfies, music, and every possible form of entertainment.

It was the party's plan to start dealing with the proles. Either they would kill themselves with the poisons of choice like cigarettes, alcohol, and addictive drugs, or the unchosen hidden poisons the party planted in the soil. They actually took poisons from gas chambers in WWII to poison soils for use as "pesticides". Most of the food grown in 2022 is poisoned. Clean food is labeled as organic and costs a multitude more than regular food.

Crystal looked down at her pack of cigarettes. Grandpa George thought these would be scarce. He didn't realize what an amazing tool it was for the party to control the proles. The price continually rose like gasoline, yet somehow the poor managed to find the money for such "luxuries". Only five cigarettes remained in a pack that held twenty just this morning. Daily this dwindling pack created an untamable anxiety. Just as the starving fear of the lack of food, the drug dependent fear of lack of product. Last night was supposed to be the last, again like every day before it. The party allowed corporations to fill cigarettes with every poison imaginable and then added a warning label. The people had the right to know some of the poisons entering their bodies. What a twisted world. Let's go back to *1984*.

Yes, in 2022, people still go missing. Rarely are cases involving proles ever solved. Crime begets more crime. There's no trial, and with the media in control of the information people received, the missing people were quickly forgotten, especially the indigenous ones.

P. 27 Repairs

"Repairs, except what you could do for yourself, had to be sanctioned by remote committees which were liable to hold up even the mending of a window-pane for two years."

Anyone who has ever dealt with the Rental Tenancy Branch or enforcing their orders knows it is no small feat to stand up for tenants' rights AND have the assistance to be sure the law is followed once the order is made. Even the police rarely involve themselves with tenants' affairs, no matter how life-threatening the situation. This happened many times throughout Crystal-Dawn's life. Having moved forty-seven times in thirty-seven years, she was well experienced in both home ownership, renting, and leasing a business. Once mold and asbestos threatened her family's health. The corporation tried to hide evidence and stole various items from the home. The police did nothing. Another time, a landlord had sent Crystal a text message threatening that he was going to shoot her. The police did nothing. The proles were not of concern to the police, not even after they died.

P. 30 Children

George was greatly influenced by the actions of the Nazis in WWII and their use of children in the Youth League. In 2022, children did have the power to turn their parents in to the police with little to no evidence; however, there were greater concerns that had been built. The party could not have given such power and free rein to children as eventually, they would grow to be party members and needed to be controlled. Many of the prole children were malnourished by their parents' choice or their own. Physical appearance was of the utmost importance, and children were encouraged to be unique while simultaneously ridiculed for standing out. Their Happy apps gave them an endless variety of people to emulate. In their actions, thoughts, and words, the New Generation became "The Human Soundtrack" (p. 68). Of course, there were always variants, doers, non-doers, and takers.

Crystal-Dawn sighed. Her oldest daughter sat beside her at the desk working on grade 11 biology homework. Tempted to draw her into a conversation about what teenagers these days were like, she decided against it. There was so few hours in the day and for them, that was real stuff that needed doing. People don't want to constantly be drawn into a conversation about our society. It can be exhausting, no doubt. Looking past her thick black upswept eyeliner and spiderlike mascara, she saw a girl who wanted a future. She was learning to expand her mind about biology so she would have a better understanding of the world throughout life. Let's check.

She said she was learning the difference between common molds and sac fungi. She was unsure how it was actually related to her future experience. Crystal was curious if she would remember this when she was older.

P. 40 Reality Control

"Who controls the Past, controls the future: who controls the present, controls the past."

This correcting of history is a problem we have in 2022, that has just reached the forefront of our attention and needs to stop NOW. The Canadian government has actually set up ministries to change the Canadian history books, Legally. Just as George predicted, the party used their control of the present to change the past, to control the future.

P. 46 Statistics

If 9/11 didn't prove it, the great Covid did. There was no topic the party wasn't willing to completely fabricate, alter, or misuse for their purposes in 2022. The data overload made it impossible to cross-verify facts, and the truth was hidden by fact-checkers.

Fact-checkers were perhaps the slimiest of online predators. At least trolls were up front, outright cruel online characters, whereas fact-checkers were paid to twist any piece of information to their liking, and that was it. Firsthand accounts and evidence were dismissed as false. Any who had partaken in the sharing of such false information was ghosted. The fact-checkers were the squealers of the twenty-second century!

Crystal chuckled at her own reference. No one else in her family had even read *Animal Farm*, so who was to laugh at her literary genius? Everyone is alone. At that moment she looked up to see a young man riding an electric scooter in a long dress coat with the tails literally flapping in the wind, the only movement his stiff straight body showed as it silently sailed past. Then across him walking in the opposite direction was a homeless man, not old perhaps only double the young man's age. He pushed a bicycle, bent over with heavy bags, hanging, burdening the movements of himself and his bike.

How backward our world is! Should it not be the old man having the easier journey and the young man using the bicycle? Perhaps it just shows how burdened we become with baggage over time in our age, and it is merely the carefree, lack of responsibility of youth that creates the lack of baggage and the need for safety helmets.

Crystal-Dawn sighed. It was now 10:00 p.m. She had written nine pages and balanced her family's needs throughout the day. One was on a sleepover. Two were prepped for school the next day. One was back to calling her dad by his real name and refusing to come to visit. The activities of the other two were unknown as that was just what life was like now in 2022. Split families meant no one wanted the other to know their businesses. Anything could be used as evidence in court. The legal system was a big mess that was just one woven injustice over another is rooted deep in racism and greed.

May 2, 2022, *1984* Part II

Have you ever read a book and been so entranced by its story only to find yourself in the real world with amazing coincidences everywhere? That's what *1984* is. Page 116, "Winston picked his way up the lane through the dappled light and shade, stepping out into pools of gold wherever the boughs parted. Under the trees to the left of him the ground was misty with bluebells. The air seemed to kiss one's skin. It was the second of May."

The morning began like any usual weekday morning. Crystal was woken by one of the girls. She had coffee on, had already packed her lunch, and readied herself for school. There was an amazing pride felt over how capable these children were! As a parent, a primal fear is leaving this world with those we love unprepared for our departure from their lives financially, emotionally, and physically. Would those we love be okay without us? These kids would be just fine. Time is balanced between imparting wisdom, teaching skills, and enjoying the present. Though as of late, there had been a lot less of the latter. Between hormones, school schedules, work schedules, and friends, the older the kids get the less enjoying of the present that is to be had.

Ah, the philosophy of parenting is a book of its own. Back to the task, she must finish writing the similarities in societies from the predicted anti-utopian *1984* and now 2022.

P. 48 Media—Again!
"There was a whole chain of separate departments dealing with proletarian literature, music, drama and entertainment generally. Here were produced rubbishy newspapers containing almost nothing except sport,

crime and astrology, sensational five-cent novelettes, films oozing with sex, and sentimental songs which were composed entirely by mechanical means on a special kind of kaleidoscope known as a versificator."

I do believe George speaks complete truth in his view of the media. Their tools and methods have intensified and become more diverse, but the distraction and brainwashing of those wanting to fill their heads with nonsense were constant.

Read up to Chapter 5—Part 2

What a wonderfully fulfilling novel! Never expected the same girl Winston wanted to rape and slit her throat at the climax would be the same girl he has a love affair with! The beautiful parallels of similar forbidden love rush into existence, that of Dr. Zhivago and Lara Boris Pasternak and Anna. You seldom hear the story from the woman's point of view, selfless in the service of her love, unprotected from the outside world.

Sometimes Crystal-Dawn would get caught in her own story of experiences. It can be so easy to relate to another individual when you have similar experiences. In 2022, marriage still existed, but much like the word of God, it had been poisoned and twisted in the minds of people. Marriage meant the end of sex, love, passion, and freedom. It became a type of imprisonment physically, financially, emotionally, and materially. Once this legal union had been made, neither person was allowed physical contact with another person unless it is the offspring of the two people. The Bible suggested a man should take his wife and leave his family. People seeking to isolate their mates ran with this idea, ride or die, you and me against the world. Even extended family, loving parents blocked out from their children and great-grandchildren's lives. Financially, one's entire life earnings were tied to their mate's whim. Years of trading one's life for money was now owned and controlled by another. Love for material objects and fear of loss and the unknown captured individuals in this legal union of slavery. Most countries globally would not recognize a woman's equal human rights, so this legal union only protected the man and gave him all rights and power.

That doesn't mean people were against monogamy. They labeled it common law and those individuals were allowed to financially benefit from the tax breaks available to married individuals. That was it. However lifelong that bond of passion and love was, people would not respect the relationship much more than they do people who were dating. If someone was already in a relationship, they were still viewed as single and open to pursuit. The predators even preyed on married individuals, testing the availability of a willing participant.

Due to the displeasure experienced with marriage, it was quite common for individuals to fill their needs elsewhere.

In *Animal Farm Part II—the Machine*, relationships between individuals are symbolized by babies, for it is from relationships that babies are born and raised and how our species continues throughout time. People didn't believe they would grow to adulthood. They would typically die within a year or two so no one put effort into helping them grow. As soon as they saw signs of weakness, they gave up. It was too much work and clearly this was not the child for them. The right child would be born one day, and they would just try again. The children that did survive past infancy were typically malnourished and weak.

Crystal sighed again. She went back outside to smoke a joint and think. This issue was a touchy one for her. It was so hard not to internalize issues. She had tried to get to know people and love them so many times in her life. It was a wonder she held faith in mankind at all, so many experiences.

The nineteen years of constant Bible study filled her head with a preconceived notion of the world. *Was it really so?* She had always been taught that God's law was above man's. The purpose of life is to serve God for He is our creator, and if we are not actively serving Him right now, what could we possibly be doing that's more important?

Seriously, try justifying spending your time doing anything other than God's purpose when you have those words ringing in your head. Not to mention, we don't know the day or hour of our master's arrival, so we must ready ourselves.

It's easy to brush off such thoughts as a mere fallacy, a story not to be taken literally. There are so many reasons why the word of God has been tainted over the years. One would be considered blindly ignorant if not willing to consider all facts. If the Bible had never been changed, then why are there so many different translations?

The Jehovah's Witnesses believe a simple man, Charles Taze Russell, had the right idea when he compiled his New World Translation of the Holy Scriptures and preached a new system with some very specific damning details. Just as we are told, NOONE knows the day or hour. We are merely taught to fear it, the end. Even the words offer a reader no comfort in part 2.

Here's what people need to know about Charles's message. Like all religions, Jehovah's Witnesses are human and therefore have imperfections. Everything humans touch is with imperfection as we are imperfect. Charles himself was soon outcast from a religion of his own creation. His wife left him and applied for divorce. Upon research as an adult, it appears as though she was upset because she wanted to write articles for the *Awake* and *Watchtower* as well, and he would not let her. He wrote the articles.

Upon self-reflection of experiences within the organization, it is apparent there is definitive sexism that exists. Women are considered the "large army" as they make up the majority of members. They can "rise through the ranks" only in the ministry by committing more hours in the ministry with titles such as publisher, auxiliary pioneer, and regular pioneer. There may have been more, but in order to be a missionary, one had to be accepted into Gilead. If you were a woman, you had to be married. They would not send a single woman to Africa. She was once told women get raped in the Congo.

When in a cheeky mood, she reflected that a man can be raped just as easily as a woman, and sadly, this experience of a man forcing himself upon a woman is not isolated to Congo. It is right here in Canada. After work parties, bars, hiking trails, and online dating meetups, the list is endless. To speak up about such things is of mixed opinions. Some people will ask, "Why didn't you come forward sooner?" What proof do you have against their word? You're terrible for not coming forward sooner because countless other people could have experienced that same abuse, and you never stepped up to stop that "monster".

She smoked another cigarette.

The me-too movement was supposed to help women feel comfortable breaking their silence. Instead, it became a sea of voices screaming, "Me too!" With the rest of the world thinking, "Ah shit," here's another one. Everyone knows it exists. It's a key reason people don't ask why. It's the elephant in the room we're too scared to address properly.

Those who do are ridiculed as whistleblowers.

Crystal felt as though the world's politics play out before her very eyes in her household.

One child is so, so pure. You can see it on her glowing face. Her character is one that has not yet been broken, the poster-girl doer. She wakes at six, makes coffee for her parents, makes lunch, and gets herself ready. She sings in the kitchen while she cleans dishes from the evening before. Children like this used to be called goodie goodies—one who aimed to be good. The name was then twisted to brownnoser—one who had their nose stuck so far up someone else's buttocks from kissing it that their nose had turned brown. It creates quite the mental vision, doesn't it? It's not a good one by any means. This overdrive of achievement is evident in all doers. It was the story of the mouse that fell in the milk. The mouse that keeps kicking and keeps churning eventually turns the milk to cream and then butter and climbs its way to freedom, is it not? It is the mouse that stops kicking that drowns.

The options of keep trying or quit and die remain. What a sad outlook. Why could people not see that there was more than just the bucket of milk and the mouse? Ah, people were so caught up on the immediate problem before their eyes, so quick to throw a bandage on a wound without even looking for infection.

The bucket was positioned in an old barn. The exterior, though completely unnecessary in detail, was a recognizable peeling red paint, grayed by the dust upon it. Old vines climbed to the hay loft in an effort to fill the building with earwigs and spiders. Inside the barn, near the dusty cow stalls, a plastic bucket half-filled with milk sat on a dirt floor. The bucket was shaded from the heat of the day, but the sun still seemed to find a way to penetrate the old building. Everywhere you looked, sunbeams shone through the cracks and holes, illuminating the sparkling dust that filled the stagnant air.

What was this sparkle dust that filled the air?

It was GLASS and POOP and straw! There were so much glass and poop and straw!

The backdoor had been nailed shut and could not be opened. No matter how much one battered at the back door, no one would answer, and the door would not budge. Others ignored its existence and took the stairs down to the lower level. The stairs were old, small, and rickety. You could only fit one person at a time. It was a solo journey. One could hear their friend conversing, but the words were indistinguishable, lacking meaning unless one really strained to hear. You had to stop talking completely, both internally and externally to hear someone else.

Ah, the bucket, it was plastic you see so the mouse that fell in the milk was unable to climb out, very slippery walls. Perhaps if it had been a natural material like a wooden bucket, the mouse could have used the grooves in the grain of the wood for escape or perhaps chewed itself grooves to climb.

Why did no one ever mention the presence of a ROPE above the bucket?

Are you aware of the significance of ROPE in our world? It has ended and saved countless lives throughout time since its existence. It is both a lifeline and a death line depending on how you use it.

I have a magic rope.
An amazing lifeline through time
Persistence, endurance, and hope.
Effort and positivity are a necessity of mine.

Yet the end of this rope is always in sight
The end has no patience, just fury and might.
Lurking in darkness, weakness, and fear,
Crushing all that we hold so dear.
Crumbled goals and broken dreams.
These are the moments when the end of the rope is illuminated it seems.

How much can a soul withstand?

Ah, the magic of the rope we tend,
For a rope has more than just one end.
Though highly illuminated in our thoughts,
The mind it really tends to rot.
What of the other end, never in sight?
For it is within you, give it some light.
This Magic Rope you see,
Is as long as you weave it to be.

Persistence, endurance, and Hope

Dreams purposes abound
Not all to reach fruition, another purpose found,
The fibers of your broken dreams,
Are now shared publicly on memes.
Full of Faith and Joy and Strife
Create the strongest pulp that is LIFE

Time not wasted, hope not lost,
You grew, stop suffering the cost.
Weave your rope with broken dreams
Tears and sweat will swell the seams.
Stop stalling life, fill yourself with hope.
It's what's required to build your rope.

Do you know how long it takes to churn a bucket of milk into a substance solid enough to escape from?

With a quick Google search, as knowledge was free and in great availability in 2022, it is found with perhaps some accuracy that "churning time is dependent on the starting temperature of the cream and the speed of churning. If you start with cream at 65 °F and churn at a speed of about 120–150 RPM, the total time of making butter (including draining buttermilk and molding butter) is about 20–25 minutes."

Now we need to know what RPM's a mouse can churn…

Mouse facts—there are many previously unknown facts that affect the parable of this story.

How long can a mouse swim for compared to that of a human?

Amazingly, they can tread water for as long as three days. One of the most impressive feats of these animals is that once they are completely underwater, they are still able to survive by holding their breath for about three minutes. Despite the fact that mice are very good swimmers, they do not really seem to enjoy swimming at all.

They can jump up to almost twelve inches from the floor.

They can run off at an astonishing speed of 8 mph.

Peta materials help educate one on the "Forced Swim Test". At first glance, it is assumed it is scientists learning how fast a mouse can paddle. Then the insidious side comes out. They are waiting for the moment the mouse stops trying. Does it mean the mouse has accepted its fate? Does it mean the mouse is reserving energy to survive? What a sick, cruel world that one would experiment on the lesser lives.

All lives matter.

A shudder ran through Crystal's body. Those were powerful words these days. To suggest such things was to suggest that one did not believe that black lives mattered. Those were racists in society. The back door swung open and thudded closed. Gerrasimos needed help in the yard.

It had been a long day and nearing 3:30 p.m. It doesn't sound late, but it sure felt it. It felt like bedtime. She pondered whether a nap would help or ruin the day. There was no way to know. Earlier in the day, the children were dropped off at school, and Crystal and Gerrasimos met his mother at his grandmother's old nursing home. Two of the children had worked here prior to Covid mandates for vaccines. They had to resign, understandably so. These are the most vulnerable of our population. They needed protection. Did they need to be locked away for their protection though?

They were clearing out the old furniture as Grandma had been moved to a high level of care home after her month-long hospital stay. She had only been feeling nauseous one day, and they figured it was anxiety from having her old chair removed and a new one put in. She never even got to sit in the chair before she was taken to the emergency. Everyone in the hospital had to wear masks. You could enter whether you were vaccinated or not, but only one vaccinated visitor was allowed to pass by the emergency doors if not suffering from an emergency themselves. Grandma shared a room with an elderly man with dementia. He would ramble on about random topics that seemed outlandish for someone with his frail body and predicament. He would speak to his daughter on the phone as she was unvaccinated and unallowed to visit. He was eventually confined to his bed as he kept trying to walk the halls, not during Covid. No one was to walk the halls but the staff. Mom would bring Grandma meals. That was until another Covid outbreak, and the floor would be so restricted they wouldn't allow healthy food to be brought in.

Food

Oh, the joy it brings to some people! It is supposed to be a necessary nutritional requirement for the body, but the party had twisted it so! Despite the new beliefs, the old traditional ones still held strong to the old ways. Mom was the matriarch of a Greek family. She was not Greek herself but a young Canadian girl who had grown up working on a farm and left at fourteen to work as the main camp cook for her father's logging operation up Shuswap Valley. Crystal loved hearing Mom's stories. They worked so hard! Anyways she married a handsome, mysterious older Greek man, which back in the 1970s was quite something. Not only were there huge cultural differences but also many businesses needed to be run and children to be raised. There were mostly restaurants, but they also had a nightclub in Vernon for some time too. Apparently, nightclubs switch hands frequently for a fresh look to attract new people.

Gerrasimos was raised with a plethora of food. Many of the Greek themes in *My Big Fat Greek*

Wedding are completely correct. It's being lost with the younger generations though. The only remnants that remain are the containers of Tzatziki in the fridge and the old Greek men that still meet. Like Simon and Garfunkle, old men, they sit and stare and talk. Mostly now in their seventies, having survived so many life-threatening illnesses, yet their weakening bodies hold on day by day. Crystal felt pain standing at the age of thirty-seven. She could not imagine the pain of a body of eighty years of life.

One cigarette was left. Will this be the one? It better be. The clerk at the store last night had a particular distaste for smokers. She had seen his eyes roll when random strangers asked for a pack. She now pondered if perhaps his ex-wife had been a smoker or a parent? Hell, maybe even one of his kids, he did say he was a grandfather of a few. Anyways, his hatred for smokers equates to not aiming to please the customer which equates to Crystal smoking bold extra. Ewww, it's terrible, smells stronger and more unpleasant experience than it ever was, to begin with.

Crystal-Dawn had taken a spiritual journey with her partner what must be a week ago now. They traveled to Dunn Lake, British Columbia. Their new slogan would be, been there, done that. And they would return home from their journey completely healed of that which burdens them. Crystal needed to be away from the temptation of cigarettes. Gerrasimos needed to find out what was holding him back from the things he knew he wanted. At twelve, he woke before daylight to bicycle himself to the pool for early morning practice. He was going to the Olympics. I believe he had it in him. He started a swim team for his high school and excelled at academics. Many athletes are not dumb jocks. They are individuals with a great wealth of knowledge about the biology of the human body.

Crystal-Dawn put out the last cigarette and gave her daughter a hug goodbye. While this sounds dramatic, it was entirely true as her daughter was leaving to ride her bicycle to the rock-climbing gym. She was awesome like that. The last purchased pack of cigarettes was almost discarded. After careful deliberation, it was decided if this was to be significant, it must be made significant.

The empty pack was placed in a scrapbook for future memory recording. FMR is a technique used for individuals who want to remember their life experiences in a beautiful, easy-to-view-and-read format. In 2022, most have moved on to digital memory savers, but a rare few still exist that scrapbook. It was this idea of a digital future memory recording that was used in the future to not only resurrect the dead but also immortalize mankind.

Crystal looked at the joint between her tanned, scarred fingers. *Eighth of an inch left,* she thought. Be wary. It must be said that you would assume that when one had the answers to mankind's problems and were writing these solutions in a book. The book would spew forth with such intensity the writer would be in a mental frenzy like *Alice in Wonderland's* rabbit that never has enough time and is always late for a very important date! It is not so.

Yes, the words were there and ready to pour forth whenever given the opportunity. Crystal was never at a loss of words. With a partner, six children, an art studio, and a big Greek family, there was always something needing attention, requiring energy.

Even now she multitasked between writing and speaking with her daughter about how to make good friends. It was a balance. Crystal had been self-employed for a long time, and the children were used to approaching and making requests at any time. It was only when Crystal was working with scalpels, the fleshing machine, or drills, did they sometimes wait until it was safe to do so. Many minor injuries occurred throughout the children's upbringing as Crystal multitasked her way through life.

Gerrasimos was off to his brothers to help unload new windows, so it was the perfect time to sit and get some writing done.

P. 55—Newspeak—A Common Language for Mankind?

In *1984* they have destroyed language to a simplified version. While a language all mankind could understand is dreamed of, yet still to be instigated, this simplified language was not what people wanted.

"It's a beautiful thing, the destruction of words. Of course the great wastage is in the verbs and adjectives, but there are hundreds of nouns that can be got rid of as well. It isn't only the synonyms; there are also the antonyms. After all, what justification is there for a word which is simply the opposite of some other word? A word contains its opposite in itself. Take 'good', for instance. If you have a word like 'good', what need is there for a word like 'bad'? 'Ungood' will do just as well—better, because it's an exact opposite, which the other is not."

In 2022, we have a twisted use for words now that do confuse the masses. This confusion typically results in the offense. Once an offense has been committed and an individual has felt offended, a series of disciplinary measures can be taken. These laws were originally intended to stop hate, racism, and division among people. They were now twisted and used for mere inexcusable, sometimes accidental or ignorant offenses. They ranged in seriousness, of course. Sometimes it was a "look", glance, or stare. The worst misuse was when people had differing opinions. If you disagreed with someone's opinion and stated something different, you were met with hate. It was mostly fueled by ignorance. Speaking of which, ironically it's perfect timing—right in line.

P. 58—George Orwell predicted Justin Trudeau in 1984

"What was slightly horrible, was that from the stream of sound that poured out of his mouth it was almost impossible to distinguish a single word. . . . As he watched the eyeless face with the jaw moving rapidly up and down, Winston had a curious feeling that this was not a real human being but some kind of dummy. It was not the man's brain that was speaking, it was his larynx. The stuff that was coming out of him consisted of words, but it was not speech in the true sense: it was a noise uttered in unconsciousness, like the quacking of a duck."

At 5:40 p.m., hunger becomes evident as something to not be ignored. It was usually around dinner time that Crystal allowed herself to eat. Food was a struggle for proles and become a huge global issue needing resolving before mankind destroyed itself or the planet.

Taking a big breath and little bites, she has to practice a little being at that moment, mindful eating and enjoying the food.

Gerrasimos was so awesome with the food. All that Olympic training and open access to his parents' kitchen equaled a man with a ferocious appetite! His body truly was a machine that needed fuel though. He did the majority of the household cooking. The children really put in effort sometimes, but that was more like the ebb and flow of the sea, sometimes there, sometimes not. He really cared about making sure the whole family was eating what their bodies needed. The majority of evenings were spent watching curiosity stream, so it became increasingly difficult to eat typical prole food knowing the poisons that were in it. People that are not the primary cooker of the nutrition for the family cannot understand the time, effort, forethought, or financial limitations that are required to create meals daily. People not only eat daily, they eat three times a day on average in 2022 and also snack between meals.

That's only in some households—globally. Whether in capitalist Canada or corrupt Cameroon, there are those that go without food daily. From children to seniors, all cities and towns. The rich and poor are no longer divided but seen sharing the same world.

Movie stars live right here in the Okanagan Valley. Crystal even provided props for a film called *The Recall* with Wesley Snipes. She brought her children and they toured the film set. The alien suit was awesome.

It was at 9:40 p.m. that the workday finished, and Gerrasimos finally came inside. He made some amazing progress on the Rainbow Natural Art Studio sign. The book *1984* leaves off at part 2 chapter 6.

There are sixteen pages written in total in two days.

May 3, 2022

A cool damp air swirls through the Okanagan Valley. It has not rained yet, but the unsettled feeling of rain was carried by the cool winds. At eight o'clock, one child was off to school, two homesick, and the other three presumably fine though currently unknown.

Today Gerrasimos and Crystal-Dawn would travel to the Kootenays to pick up building materials for their new house. It was unheard of for a prole to build their own home as materials costs soared far beyond anything ever once thought reasonable. Only members of the inner party could build a home. Even then they couldn't actually afford it. It was just a means of becoming indebted to the banks.

Wood had tripled in value, hardware, and even tools. Scavenging was the only way to find affordable building materials. They were traveling to acquire trusses from an old airport hangar. This would serve as the greenhouse roof for their future home.

Gerrasimos was stirred from sleep, and it was time to go. Men had an amazing ability to wake and immediately begin their day. Women typically needed an hour at least to ready themselves.

George thought women wouldn't wear makeup in the future because it created desire. Little did he know women would be controlled by it. The problem with makeup was that it became more common than sugar. It was no longer a means for a woman to dress up. For school, work, and even running errands, makeup became as necessary as the masks of the Covid. Makeup disguised a person so that if seen without it, it would frighten many. Animals were cruelly tested to ensure the makeup had minimal, short-term, negative effects. Gender is a whole 'nother issue but not for today.

This was uniquely terrible. Straight up, tear spewing terrible. Did you know *1984* has a book within a book? Crystal had gotten to *The Theory and Practice of Oligarchical Collectivism*.

It is difficult to express the level of anticipation Crystal felt over finding this gem. It was as though the rest of this wonderful book had been filler leading up to this one amazing part. Surely George couldn't have published it by himself or the powers that be would have never let it into existence. It was no wonder *The Theory and Practice of Oligarchical Collectivism* was never created into a film so the proles could watch and learn. George must have been extremely intelligent for his writings were complicated and contained many unused words in 2022. Gerrasimos was also an intelligent man and helped explain some of the meanings and pronunciations. Homeschoolers rarely pronounced words correctly as they had read it themselves. Language was to be written and spoken, but sometimes the words did not match up, especially in the English language.

So Crystal-Dawn began reading out loud throughout the journey. A conversation was ignited about the sinking ship our society was. People had differing points of view. In theory, there's nothing wrong with a person thinking about what they choose. He was free to think that the ship was sinking and they had to save themselves. The problem occurred with the ship. Crystal's mind was far too vivid with imagining scenarios to their finest detail. A vision could develop and shift shapes between different symbolisms to "see" the scenario.

The ship shifted between an old wooden pirate ship once used to create trade between countries, then twisted to deliver a cargo of enslaved humans and the glorious *Titanic*. An invention again of man's making, the *Titanic* boasted the best the world could create at the time.

Whether it be a pirate ship or the *Titanic*, the same visual remained—bad people were seen on the main deck, partying and not giving care for the impending doom they faced. We know in the case of *Titanic*, these "first-class", inner-party people had warnings. They had the means to escape safely and choose not to because they were comfortable. We also know at the same time the boat was sinking, they were dancing on the corpses of those on the lower floors, locked below deck with no choice for escape.

Crystal-Dawn began crying and Gerrasimos just didn't understand why. She kept saying, "You won't even look in the hull!" He most definitely did not share the same vision as Crystal. He felt that the ship was sinking, and it was in his ability to build a new ship for their family. In reality that meant building their home and moving out to raw land where they could be prepared for whatever future befalls mankind. Crystal loved and appreciated Gerrasimos for being the practical one, sound in mind. His self-preservation would help them all. He believed as in a crashing flight, you need to put your air mask on before helping others. Crystal-Dawn fell under a different train of thought where everything else came first, and by helping others, she in turn would also be elevated with everyone. Many individuals were frustrated with the current system of things and were just waiting for it to go up in flames. Crystal understood the feeling.

> I'm so sick of me, being sick of you, and the way you look, all the things you do,
> You drive me crazy, drive me crazy.
> Sick of being broke, can't pay for shit, I'm about to snap, I can't handle this,
> I'm going crazy, doing crazy (Going crazy)
> If you're sick like me, there's no stopping now, try to break it up, and just let it out.
> If I was sick like you I would feed the fire, I would light it up and watch it all drop down.
> (Adelitas Way, "Sick")

She was sick of it too. But the idea of letting it go up in flames or sink to the icy waters below was not an option.

The hull. She had to Google the meaning as she wasn't a boat person and was entirely unsure if the hull was even the correct word. She just knew what was under the deck of the ship. Each time the old wooden safety hatch was lifted it was the same sight. It was the Vulnerable. Already surrounded by water, some bodies already drowned with lifeless white eyes staring in every direction, their bodies buoyed. Some old, some young, every race and gender was equally trapped beneath the floor. Rats swam among the people spreading disease and death. Their beady eyes stared from every corner of the room. To the rats, they knew the danger, and they viewed this hull as their playground and dining room, a personal Chucky Cheese of sorts complete with food and water! It was as if staring into a raccoon den where the mother hadn't returned for several days, and the babies were far past anticipating her arrival. Some had died; some had begun eating their siblings. They had lost hope their mother would ever return until the light came streaming in through the open hatch.

Their faces were a blend of confusion, shame, pain, and anger. No actual smiles of hope could be found. Maybe they thought they dreamed of it so many times before. Perhaps they mistook the light for their cruel masters returning. Can you imagine being so accustomed to the dark the light was feared?

Either way, the sea of Vulnerable, both living and dead, looked up from the hull of the ship. They couldn't escape. Some didn't even want to. Despite deadly conditions, some chose not to leave. The young ones had been born here and never knew of anything different. How were they to have hope if they had never experienced anything different? Life was either bad, worse, or unbearable.

Could people really look at this ship, whether an old pirate ship or the glorious *Titanic* and condemn it to death without even looking at the Vulnerable that went down with it?

Mamoushka's face was always in the crowd. Everywhere there was a Vulnerable, there was Mamoushka.

The Machine
There is so much to be said. It is most difficult to stick to one train of thought and ignore the presence of others. You see it is in thinking that these connections are made. By letting the mind flow and wander where it will. Crystal-Dawn stopped reading when Winston told Julia he had the book and she said, "That's nice, dear," and it didn't come up again for another half an hour. He excitedly told her the amazing power of this book and that all should read it! Just as she was saying to Gerrasimos. Then Julia sleepily suggested that he read it so she could listen and hear of it. Crystal glanced over at Gerrasimos driving, waiting to hear the next page.

It was eerily similar. She had not once flipped ahead in the book to learn of the future, but in this instance, she just had to know.

Yup, just as suspected, Julia had fallen asleep after what seemed like a good three pages of pure world-changing goodness. THESE were the words that explained our society, how it truly is, and how it can be fixed. What could possibly be more important? Surely just as Winston had believed, everyone needed to hear these words, and so too Crystal had to ensure all knew this truth.

Strangely enough, George refers to the machine. Perhaps somewhere in her time, Crystal had already heard this phrase. Maybe it existed in the pages of *Animal Farm*. In *Animal Farm Part II—the Machine*, Crystal thought she had been original in her idea that once pigs and men had reached an alliance, they created a machine together.

This machine would be "sustainable"

- able to be maintained at a certain rate or level.
- able to be upheld or defended.

And it is run by the people, all the people, the inner party, outer party, and proles. All of society was the energy running the machine.

It was not sustainable though as the Earth did not carry enough resources for such consumption of goods. There was enough for all, but to maintain the machine, large amounts of resources had to be disposed of through war just as a fire needs fuel and air and heat. There doesn't need to be a spark; it could be an intense amount of energy. Spontaneous combustion from the amount of heat produced by the machine started fires everywhere. Wars and disputes broke out continually, both internationally and within one's own home.

The Earth could be explained in mythology as a celestial woman that one day, along with her family, curled up for a long restful slumber. The sun, her father, warmed her in favor. Other siblings were closer, and some more distant from their father, but all held within his immense gravitational pull. The energy of the father, the sun, is great you see. So great was he, yet even he had an impending collapse one day. The entire family slowly separated from one another in what was perceived to be inevitable entropy.

The earth was the most favored of the celestial children. This favor bore LIFE. Life was energy made possible by everything. The entire fabric of the universe was within every living being. Carbon made their bodies. Hydrogen and oxygen created the water that flowed through the veins of everything. A web covered the womanlike skin in a protective, sensitive, connected layer of nerves. It was the fungi. Just as mites cover a person's skin to remove dead cells, the fungi too protected the woman and cleansed her of the dead upon her.

The humans on the surface of the Earth were the fastest to evolve. The woman provided everything that all species dependent on it needed to survive. Some recognized her as Mother Earth and celebrated her natural beauty and medicine. The Earth WAS sustainable and any species that were not go extinct.

Mankind was on the extinction list and was already considered the walking dead. The people had become zombies and literally attacked and killed anyone with an opposing thought. Much like the thought police of *1984*, Karen's enforced the "common belief"—more their own reality projected upon the world with great loud voices and much-taken offense. Although recognized for being irrational and actually despised, they maintained their position and continued to spread hate, taking personal offense to all those contrary in opinion.

Oh, the machine! So you see, when men and pigs came together to create this "sustainable" machine, they had in fact unearthed or mutilated Mother Earth to expose her heart. Like a comatose patient, she lay breathing heavily pained breaths from the poisons they filled her lungs with. The water that ran through her veins was poisoned, and her body struggled to fight off the infection. Her blood could only filter so much at a time, and mankind was waterboarding her. Would you believe mankind, still unable to explore her depths, still manages to scrape the insides of her womb for cysts, more and more eliminating any chance for reproduction and rebirth? They slaughter the children of her womb with no other excuse other than man's greed. They disguise it as a need for food. Proles are sent out in the most dangerous of conditions. All are chained to the pirate ship in an endless servitude of death and destruction. Were they ever given the chance to see something better? Were there other, safer jobs available to these people that raped the Earth and killed her children? Were there other means available to feed their bellies and survive?

No.

The proles were not helped by the people of the world and continued running the machine, raping and pillaging the woman, not by choice but by a need for survival.

Crystal stopped writing. It was the heart that was the key. She would need Gerrasimos and his knowledge of biology to help explain to the people what had happened to the Earth's heart. For when the truth was revealed and the animals found what men and pigs had done, they were going to need it explained in a way that touched the common understanding of everyone.

The heart had been mined about it and lay in an open deep pit surrounded by scaffolding to reach all around. All parts could be accessed from these scaffolds. It sounds shabby, but they had placed a facade on the fronts so as to make it appear attractive.

The heart was clearly dying if it had not already died a long while back. It was kept alive with artificial means. Hoses attached here and there, and the resonating thud was not that of a human heart at rest but that of a frightened animal. It was not a natural pulse but a forced, machine-driven pulse, that of a steam engine that with each forced push there was a guaranteed forced pull.

The heart had long ago begun to spring leaks and was quickly bandaged. They never asked why the damage occurred but sought only to fix the immediate problem before them. That was mankind's problem, don't you know? They recognized the problems and either chose not to look at them and rely on the self-healing powers of the heart, or they sought a means to bandage it as quickly as possible for the purposes of maintaining the machine.

Mankind was like that. Shutdowns were created because so much waste was produced throughout production that it became a fire hazard. As minimally as possible, once a year, a special staff was brought in to work around the clock in shifts to repair and clean as much as possible within that given time frame.

There was never enough work done to properly fix anything, just bandages. The bandages eventually festered into tumors, some were benign, some malignant. The malignant tumors became metastatic and traveled throughout the whole body of Mother Earth.

Now the problem was in 2022 that it was said not one man could do all the tasks required to do something as simple as creating a pencil. And it was true! Something as complicated as the removal of tumors from a heart, they had not fully gained an understanding of would surely lead to the death of the patient. The patient dies, and all lifeforms dependent on her die too.

The surgery was far too risky for anyone to even consider. To consider such things was illegal and labeled as treason and inciting violence and destruction. Granted this belief was only held by those in power, those of the smallest minority in power and spread throughout society.

This surgery was required for the survival of everything and would require every person of every specialty on Earth to perform.

Somewhere in the Bronze Age, between 4500–800 BC, people began an urban revolution. There began densely populated areas, social class structures, taxation, trade, monumental building, writing, and specialized occupations. These specialized occupations divided mankind to a degree. We are in 2022 when no one can create a simple pencil by themselves. This is why it was required for all mankind to come together in this effort to save the heart. The tumors of crumbling organizations, once used as a bandage to solve a problem, now created a greater problem with their decayed presence. Religion with its ability to heal became corrupted by resources and became one of the metastatic tumors. The sun had repeatedly sent solar flares throughout time, shooting charged particles toward the Earth. Coronal mass ejections set the stage for change. The people grew restless, sparky, revolutionary, and curious; they were ready for change! Did you know high peaks of solar activity are recorded around the French Revolution, the American Revolution, and the 1960s? Did you also know on the Easter of 2022 the sun emitted a massive coronal mass ejection? It was registered as an X1.1-class sun storm (X-class storms are rated as the most powerful). It lasted for a whole half hour. The sun is currently in the fourth year of an increasingly active phase of an eleven-year solar weather cycle.

The 144, 000 souls had risen from the Earth in an effort to help people, help the Earth, and create positive change. Those who shone with the light of truth were evident to those around them. They were met with the extremists of our world because they preached balance and equality, love for all, and an end to this system of things. The inner-party minority did not want the system to end. As George Orwell explains, the upper class doesn't want things to change. The middle class wants to become the upper class and occasionally manages to do so. The lower class never sees change but dreams of equality for all.

"Hope lay with the Proles"

The proles did not have the specialty skills required to fix the heart and believed the lie that any existence outside this current reality would end in bloodshed. Films like the purge were created to literally show the proles how bad it would be.

It was also the truth, but it lacked one key component the upper class had not yet crushed.

Love of Neighbor

The people were not actually blood-hungry savages. They were people. Every individual mattered and was hurting beyond anyone's comprehension but their own. They were so burdened by daily life they could not take on the weight of another. Some still tried.

Crystal-Dawn stopped writing again, not intentionally as the laptop battery had died and stopped short the brilliance that spewed forth from her mind if only people would listen to her. Only an hour remained, and she needed to leave for a trip to Kelowna. Today they were meeting with Gerrasimos's sister. They had milled some old CN Railway ties to smaller dimensions for fence posts and were being contracted to do the work of erecting a fence. The posts were mostly oak, some red oak, and maple. It was the most amazing wood to be laid on the ground as a railway tie. At least they were able to salvage the rejects and reuse them for a good purpose. His sister had just returned from a trip to Belize, South America, where they had purchased some property and intended to build a vacation home. Being the tradespeople of the family, it was likely that Gerrasimos and Crystal-Dawn could assist with building it. They had already helped renovate the living room and were building a fence, so it was no small feat of the imagination that perhaps one day they would be on a flight to Belize, escorted through an island, and spend the next few weeks moving brush and building with what materials are available. That was one of the amazing things about Gerrasimos. He could build anything with anything. He was a true natural MacGyver, crossed with a thrifty man that preferred to reuse materials or create his own from raw materials. Crystal-Dawn was quite the do-it-yourselfer as well as a self-taught taxidermist and valued this amazing man. Despite what may have appeared to be a disorganized hoarder of useless things, he was in fact a saver and repurposer of things.

Those were the best kind of people in our world, the ones that don't need to consume more and new. The ones that value the old and know the energy required to create new. There is so much waste these days, overconsumption of goods and resources. He told Crystal-Dawn there were two types of engineers, one who created something for the purpose of breaking, the most despicable kind, and the one who created something to last forever. These people were scarce as it meant the customer would not return for repairs. Warranties would be useless, and the machine would not be fed its toll.

Ah, the machine! With such frustration, Crystal stared at the now slightly ratty *1984* book on the desk. Its front cover was now slightly ripped standing three inches in the air. It wanted to be read. It needed to be finished. She hadn't picked it up since she found out Julia had fallen asleep while being read to. It was exasperating and left her wondering, *What's the point?* If no one cares to hear, then what is the point. It would take all people on Earth to fix it. if no one would even listen, then what was the point of even trying this hard?

Those were the thoughts of hopelessness.

Crystal-Dawn recognized it and reasoned that the hopeless road was not one that she could travel.

This was Crystal's road.

As I walked along this path called life,
Something shiny caught my eye,
It glistened, calling just my sound.
With ease, I moved into its realm.
Yet capture not easy, and well sought,
Became my character's central plot.
Off the beaten path, it gleamed,
Full of peril and heartache it seemed.

Was it worth the price so dear,
Or was it just desire's fear?

Obsession carries a heavy cost,
All other interests are seemingly lost.
And what if the object you hold so dear
Is nothing more than a shiny mirror?
For it is within ourselves we long,
To obtain our own siren song.

Passions pursued, time beautifully spent,
the treasures within us, won't cost you a cent.

It was 10:30 p.m. Back from Kelowna. Turns out Crystal had misunderstood the trip. It was not to discuss their involvement in Belize. There was no mention of it, but rather the detailed plans from a construction company that would complete the work. It was part of the purchase agreement to use a contractor. Crystal was merely there to build a fence, labor. Thankfully, when she was at her lowest, Gerrasimos always tried to help pick her up again. He gave encouraging words that they would rather be the builders of the world. They had spoken of their love for work for so long. She lay across him, over, under, and through as he gingerly rubbed her back. A few tears fell. He got it. He knew. He had been raised in a family a few steps above the lowest rung, so he had never been in want. He had completed a degree with fabulous grades, started a vehicle import company, and rebuilt his favorite car to be electric all before he was thirty. He owned houses; he traveled the world. That was all before his experience. Most people have experienced enough by their forties to give an idea of what life is really like. Some are jaded, few are hopeful, but most are indifferent as they strive to thrive and survive. Gerrasimos had lost his business, and both homes got swallowed up in relationship separations with nothing to show in the end except a semi container of old furniture and a few vehicles in a farm field that couldn't be registered. He was someone that had the most beautiful soul and incredible drive and had been reduced to forced full-time employment selling gasoline vehicles. The once president of the Vancouver Electric Vehicle Association had been a visionary of the next generation's sustainable future and was now selling gas-guzzling cars. A trip to burning man had freed his soul. Burning man had that power, don't you know? It is not what it used to be and never will be again, but small burns will rise globally. They are the rainbow warriors of the native American prophecy.

May 4, 2022
9:00 a.m.

Crystal-Dawn sat at the desk outside their bedroom box. Their room was simply a bed-sized "box", composed of a bed and a cedar shelving unit to one side. It was exactly what they needed and not an inch more. Gerrasimos was telling her what social life was like in Greece. In the evenings the streets would come alive with so many people it was thought impossible so many could fit on one island. Where had all these people been during the day? There were old men smoking pipes and sipping drinks, children running and playing. It just appeared so natural. Girls strutted their stuff on display. There were no high, rises and business suits that he had once thought were the echelon of doctors and lawyers and businesspeople. He had been told that was the ideal to reach—suits, company directors, stock markets, and banks. The wizards of our world when they come out from behind the curtain they're usually well dressed.

He beckoned her back to bed again. After another beautiful beginning to the day, they collapsed in exhaustion. He picked up her binder on positive psychology. She had brought home her old therapy binder last night and pointed out the 5:1 positivity ratio for Gerrasimos to read. Dr. Rick Hanson, a neuroscientist from Berkley University had written an amazing article on "Do positive experiences stick to your ribs?" He probably wasn't expecting his words would be read in the most loving and positive of experiences, but it was most delightful to hear Gerrasimos read aloud about the human brain and its inner workings. He liked the idea of a "wise mind"—the experience of being in touch with your emotions while at the same time having the capacity to think logically while making decisions, going within to integrate an emotional mind and reasonable mind.

A wise mind is part of each of us so that we can know and experience truth. It integrates all ways of knowing. The "magic" of intuition. The calm that follows the storm. When you grasp the whole picture and know something directly and clearly.

Crystal-Dawn was far beyond ecstatic that Gerrasimos was taking such an interest. He was not only reading aloud, he was analyzing his own experiences and that of our society. Negative experiences trump positive ones. He went off on trump. Apparently, the politician Trump has taken the meaning of this word as we cannot read through a sentence with the word trump holding its original meaning.

It was a slaughter of words.

Crystal-Dawn tried to get more reading done. She began part 3, realizing this entire portion of the book was torture. Literally, both for the character and the reader. Winston had been caught by the thought police, pages upon pages of torture. Most difficult to read but necessary. There was a reason George had written it. She was able to pull the gems of truth hidden amongst the pain. Did you know it was Winston's brotherhood contact that turned out to be his torturer? He had provided him with the book that would offer truth, and then page after page, unknown days of pure torture to break the truth from him. Why? It's because they saw in his resistance to their ways and could not merely end his life and create a martyr. They had to crush him first, not just physically with the torture and not just with a confession but with a true inner crushing of his belief would they then succeed and could end his life.

The reality was far too painful to read. Crystal-Dawn too many times throughout her life had stood up for what was right. That was usually the decimating move. You see when she smiled and spoke fondly of the party, they loved her. They saw her light and wanted to shine it positively on their works, which surely there is good and bad in everything. Anyone can look at the good or the bad. They both existed simultaneously. She had once been permanently recorded in Canadian history, in a Hansard report, for being a hard-working diligent trade worker. When she came upon rough waters, they were nowhere to be found. These people were not in the business of solving problems. That wasn't capitalism. There was a huge rift in the treatment of trade students and academic students, but it was not a rift the colleges were willing to address.

When she was younger, a girl of nineteen, she had attended her first year of studies at Selkirk College in Castlegar, British Columbia. Sociology, geomorphology, history, English, and computer science, everything was fascinating. There are many people in our world that would love to spend their lives studying, learning, and filling themselves with all the knowledge of the world. They are labeled as "Van Wilders" and suggested they merely want to party. A lifelong passion for academics and study must be funded by someone. These students eventually became paid professors because they needed the universities to fund their studies. Teaching students was just a side burden placed upon professors that did not want to teach.

In an English class, some blonde girls were chatting a row behind Crystal, sharing stories of recent travels. One had returned from what she called "Hongcouver." A derogatory term used for the city of Vancouver suggests so many Chinese people had moved there. It was now another Hong Kong. What these girls failed to realize in their absent-minded bigotry was that a row behind them silently sat two international students. Clearly of Asian descent, these two quiet girls sat in the back listening to the blonde girls before them speak. Crystal-Dawn was disgusted with such outward racism. She spoke to the teacher after class and was told there wasn't much he could do about it, more injustice. Crystal-Dawn quit going to the class and never passed it. In retrospect, the class had cost over $500 toward a student loan she still owed money on. If she had paid cash for the class with her earnings from her four jobs she simultaneously juggled, she would have appreciated the value and not dropped out due to others' hatred. She would have stood up to the girls and told them to take that bigotry and get the fuck out. We always have so much nerve and gumption after the fact, eh? (This Canadian usage of the nonword "eh" indicates the speaker is checking with the listener if they are in agreeance.) Most people can relate to being frozen in fear when action or words are required. The fear was crippling.

Have you ever heard the term "stunned cunt"? It is typically used by trades workers, the proles, to insult a woman, but just as every other insult is directed toward women, it could be directed at anybody. What was a stunned cunt though? Drawing from her own life experience, Crystal-Dawn would define a stunned cunt as the moment a man hits a woman, and she lies on the ground unreactive. She is not knocked out cold though. Rather she is in a state of disbelief and frozen in terror as to how to respond. Should she respond as one should when being hit by another individual? Are we not supposed to yell, scream, fight back, run to safety, and call the police? Apparently not leading up to 2022. Police are rarely called. As a side note, while we are drawing from personal experience of a man hitting a woman, this is not always the case. There are far too many women that think it's OK to hit a man, whether in a state of frustration, jokingly, or impaired with alcohol or other mind-altering substances. Now with the new world of 2022, what happens when an individual with the physical, biological makeup of a man but now identifies as a woman hits a woman? Do the same laws apply that this was an unfair abuse of power, or is it now matched as less significant as the current society has odd, sexual ideologies of a woman and a woman fighting. Surely the impact of being hit by one's partner is no less significant?

But WHY, why would someone lay there conscious, stunned in submission?

Disbelief. The person who is supposed to love you, care for you, support you, just hurt you. Will they do it again? If you get up, will it anger them? What must you have done to trigger THAT? Even after they leave the room and you're alone, do you call the police? Well, chances are if the police came, that would mean the children would see them; they would see menacing, puffed-out tall bullet-proof men armed with guns. Americans were used to seeing handguns everywhere, so they carried less of a fear of guns. Canada was different though. Handguns were restricted firearms. For the average citizen that was allowed a restricted firearms license, the rules were so strict that the average citizen never knew of them. They could only be transported to and from a shooting range at a gun club in a locked case. The only time a handgun was seen by a Canadian citizen, it was prominently displayed on the hip of a police officer, a conservation officer, or an armed security guard.

These individuals had such an immense presence. It was terrifying to be around one. There was a time, locked away in Crystal's youthful memories, when her father had been extremely proud of carrying a firearm as a Brinks security guard in Calgary, Alberta. He had always been a trucker, and Brinks offered an opportunity for a trucker to carry a gun, have a uniform that demanded a level of respect, and a decent wage. It was not much better than that of a long-haul trucker, and the danger was far more imminent. He loved it and her Jehovah's Witness mother hated it. During their separation, he drank a lot. His sister worried for him. He would park outside the bar with his Brinks uniform hung in his window. That way when the police approached his vehicle and saw him sleeping within, they would not disturb him or question him. Bloody smart man he was. He volunteered for the Calgary Police and bore a volunteer ID. This he kept at the forefront of his wallet in case he ever needed to open it for the police. He wasn't just a sneaky, smart person; he was a good person within—a frustrated, sometimes angry, mostly fighting trucker. You know he was once charged by the police for pulling his tractor-trailer up behind the car that had suddenly cut him off. He didn't just stop behind him. Oh no, he got out with a weapon in hand. The plaintiff said he had been threatened and his vehicle kicked and dented by steel-toe boots. Crystal's father wore Hush Puppies, a soft slipper that made driving long distances more bearable. It was impossible that what he had been charged with had occurred. However, it was this one event that sent his life spiraling down the hole of unemployment, health failure, foreclosure, possessions taken to the dump, attempted suicide by stepping in front of another driver's tractor-trailer, hospitalization, homelessness, and when he finally pulled up on the reins of his life and had acquired a home in Drumheller, Alberta, he had a stroke.

Crystal-Dawn sat and contemplated on her father. He was currently a wolverine, for real. When he died, he wanted to be cremated, and she was allowed to keep the ashes. A wolverine had been acquired by a trapper in Manitoba. It had magnificent colors and bore a heart on its backside. Crystal created a space within the wolverine's body to house her father's ashes. He currently sits in her showroom with no tongue, as a political statement for the truckers of Canada. What better than a wolverine to represent a strong, fighting working class? In reality, he never let her get a word in edgewise, so it was now quite fitting that he was bound to silently listen.

Geez, she scrolled back up. How had she started thinking about her father again? This was supposed to be explaining the definition of stunned cunt. If you haven't already recognized the lucid connectedness that occurs in Crystal's writings while shifting from one idea to another, it still has enough substance to hold together as a complete, fully evolved belief system that people are worth It!

Every person with their own unique story of strife and achievements, of growth and adaptation.

Crystal-Dawn had once written a poem to simply that which is the journey of life.

Desire
Longing
Energized
Pursuit
Discovery
Disinterest
Dissatisfaction
Change
Growth
Wisdom
Aging
Exhaustion
Satisfaction
Peace

The ascent
The descent
The top
The bottom

The beginning

The end

It seemed satisfactory at the least. Few of her poems ever carried the depth she wished, and the ones that did were typically left unread. She dreamed of being a poet once. When she was a teenager, she ran away every day and would trespass on the private boat launches in Summerland and sit facing north. Sitting above the waters below, Okanagan Lake spread out before her, and the sky opened to all the possibilities of the heavens. It was here in Trout Creek that she wrote beautiful poetry about the relationship between the seagulls and the water, alone, together. She wanted to be a poet like the great Dr. Zhivago! She had even used the name Tonya when working at a Safeway in Penticton behind the deli counter. No one ever pronounced it with the proper Russian energy required to properly say, Tonya. Much like *A Night at the Roxbury* calling "Emiliooo," or Rocky shouting, "Adrian!" There was a proper way to say a name and the average Canadian citizen did not know how to properly roll their tongue and soften their tone to allow the name Lara to flow from their lips, let alone the desperate cry of Tonya (pronounced Tone-Ya with the tongue curled, emphasizing on the *O* to lower the voice)!

People rarely tried to pronounce foreign-sounding names. It was common in the immigration of the thirties and forties for people to change their name to a more English-sounding name. Gerrasimos was reduced to Gerry. Can you imagine what a crushing blow it was to the soul to hear a word as beautiful as Gerrasimos reduced to Gerry? One of Crystal's adoptive mothers had been named Tuensina. It was a Dutch name, very beautiful when heard and spoken properly. It was changed but Crystal ensured the name carried on with her youngest bearing it in her middle name. It wasn't often Crystal had been allowed to name her children, but this was found to be acceptable.

It was somewhat understandable that Crystal was not entrusted with the naming of another human being as she had wanted to name the first child Meso. It was uncommon with English names, but Crystal had recently been exposed to Asian students in college and appreciated the simplicity of it. Not to mention her new married name was Short, it seemed almost meant to be! Her daughter would one day approach someone and say, "Hi! Meso Short!"

Crystal still laughed at that one, especially since the eldest child had so since proven to be of small stature. It wasn't of her own choosing though. Ever since she was eight, she had been first diagnosed with celiac disease and next Crohn's disease. She spent many years on a gluten-free diet. It was the catalyst that forced Crystal-Dawn to spend a great deal more finances on nutritional food and better feed her children than the usual gluten-filled Kraft dinner and Ichiban noodles that filled the diets of most lower-income families.

She was allowed to name the middle one. She received Jessica, for Jessica Rabbit, the sexiest cartoon ever created, middle name, Kelly. She would have picked Grace Kelly, but her ex thought it sounded religious. Grace Kelly was one of the most amazing people to "grace" the world with her presence though, so at least the Kelly was saved. Also, Crystal had a friend of that name growing up, and she was the most wonderful, endearing friend. It was actually her mom's friend, but most of her friends growing up were either her mom's or older ones in the congregation.

May 5, 2022

While there held value in all ponderings, there was a goal that was meant to be attained, and beautifully poetic language and descriptive words tell of the environment that was seen as just filler material for a book that did not require it. This was a true story, and she would simply add photographs for the readers. A picture was worth a thousand words, and people's time was the most valuable currency in their possession. She would not waste anyone's time with the extras but pondered perhaps later returning to add indented paragraphs when she did the first edit and add fluff that could be read by choice or skipped if so desired to save time reading. Time was so valuable, and people purposely wasted it these days. They wanted it to pass to the next amazing moment. This is a fact. A movie starring Adam Sandler called *Click* described this problem as did Harry Chapin's "Cats in the Cradle" song or Trace Adkin's song "You're Going to Miss This." Time flies by so fast. Everyone was aware of it. The youth dreamed of the benefits and freedoms of age. The aged dreamed of the benefits and freedoms of youth. Society was backward. The youth should have enjoyed every moment of their journey and the experiences that shaped them. These experiences were labeled as good or bad. Since psychology proves negativity leaves a far greater scar on our memory than positive experiences, as soon as an individual experiences something negative, they labeled it as bad. Eventually over time, as individuals lost hope, they labeled everything and everyone as bad. These were the individuals that needed help the most. Can you imagine living such a life? Believing everyone was out to get you, you're a helpless victim beaten by a cruel and uncaring world. The extremists of this belief carry fully loaded firearms into schools and businesses. Their personal reality of a terrible world is manifested in their actions, physically creating the terrible world in which they see.

Gerrasimos entered the room and brought Crystal back to reality. There was forty-five minutes remaining until they were due to an appointment to view a new sawmill they would be acquiring. Crystal had been excited to view this new mill, just as one would want to go to a car lot and see their new car. Unfortunately, it was raining so that removed all possibilities from crawling around on the grass around the mill to see how it looked. They currently milled large trees with the

Alaskan Chainsaw Mill but were wanting something for the smaller logs.

It had a 36-inch throat by range road, 22 hp Predator motor, 4 cycles, and a lot of other details that just confused Crystal. It used 772 watts, nothing to do with a horse. Those were the last words uttered by Gerrasimos as he went inside shutting the door behind him. He had asked what was confusing, so she read back the part about 22 horsepower and 4 cycles, and lost a good 8 minutes there. It wasn't lost. He was trying to teach her, and she was trying to write a book, smoke a joint, drink coffee, have one last cigarette, and have time to get dressed in the next half hour. Upon reflection, Crystal realized he had originally come outside to tell her he wanted to leave early so they had time to stop at his parents' home. That meant there was no longer 45 minutes left for what Crystal had imagined. The laptop was closed and she shuffled inside to get dressed as she was still in pajamas, her typical wardrobe of choice complete with a housecoat.

3:18 p.m.

The sawmills were in a box so couldn't really be "seen": however, a log cutter/splitter was set up from the same brand that they could see. The welds looked good. It was blue and faded yellow. The cutthroat was not a full 36 inches but rather 31 ½ inches, so Gerrasimos was trying to decide which would be the best purchase for this milling business they were setting up. They picked up the children from school. One needed to work almost immediately after and requested a ride, so Crystal went back to work writing while the kind and loving Gerrasimos gave her a ride. He was so awesome. Later this evening they had a planned date night to attend the local Army Navy for a game of billiards. Once a week Gerrasimos liked to join some older men to play "golf" on a pool table. Crystal had never been as apparently it was a very serious game and required ultimate concentration. She really wanted Gerrasimos to spend a little more time on the things that gave him joy, and a pool table was one of his greatest joys. He had grown up for several years as a teenager with keys to his parents' nightclub. Whenever he wanted, he could stop by after hours and play a game. Over the course of his life, he had gotten quite good! One day when they had built their dream home and were living out on the property, there would be an epic hand-carved pool table built by Gerrasimos himself. It would be elevated on a gazebo and be a central piece of furniture in their greenhouse/living room.

10:30 p.m.

On May 5, 2022, Crystal-Dawn finished reading *1984*. It neared bedtime, and Gerrasimos was already in bed with a show. There was so much to say for *1984*. Crystal-Dawn finally understood the point and exactly what she needed to do. George Orwell's writing had only further cemented her beliefs and it was now more clear than ever what she needed to do.

Tomorrow she would rise and begin the day reading *Animal Farm*. She would need a refresher of George's writing style to continue channeling his words. An abundance of words was unnecessary as the purpose of the book was not to create an elaborately detailed picture for the reader to understand. This was real life. There were photos, historical accounts, quotes, song lyrics that had been memorized long before they wizened up and began changing their words while simultaneously claiming they have never changed their beliefs.

May 6 2022.
7:30 a.m.

Crystal-Dawn begins the usual routine with caffeine, sugar, nicotine, glue, and phlegm. For seven years she had been surviving on this diet, but that was literally all it was survival. In *1984*, Winston had his teeth beaten out of him. Some fell out due to the degradation of his body, but they were replaced with dentures when the party tries to break him into submission. It was assumed George Orwell still had his teeth. Had he experienced having all his teeth removed and replaced with immediate dentures, he would have been able to go into excruciating detail about what this experience was like. Winston was brought to the edge of death with the most extreme pain possible and didn't break until the final suggested act of torture. He just wanted the pain to stop to the extent he was hoping for the peace that death offered. The final torture was a face cage with ferocious rats in it. In the Middle Ages, it was common to use rats in torture. Crystal-Dawn had once been engrossed by the misery of the Dark Ages. It was said that we are currently living in the days of the end, so it was always a curiosity to Crystal that the Dark Ages be so terrible and yet the present, which appears to be so much better, be the worst it has ever been to be considered the days of the end. A seemingly dark topic for studying, she delved into torture devices, the witch trials, and the bubonic plague. Gerrasimos didn't understand how or why she would choose to watch and learn such stomach-twisting events. She had even written a screenplay once called *The Executioner*. That was back in the days when the *Sopranos* were popular, so she wrote the lead role for James Gandolfini. When she traveled to England, she was so well versed in history that the town of York came alive in a way seen only by her. Cobblestones lined the roads and tall brick buildings grew out over into the street. Buckets were launched from windows spewing their contents on all below. Dogs, cats, horses, and people scuttled about each to their own business.

Have you ever watched people about their business in a public area? It is similar to watching an anthill with more character. Apparently only 50 percent of the ants are actually working and the other half are just wandering around looking busy. Humans pale in comparison with even less in pulling the workload.

Hope Lies with the Proles

The breaking of Winston was one simple submission in the end. He wished, in fact begged for this cruelest of tortures to be done to his love Julia. If someone could wish the worst fate possible on the person in their life with the strongest emotional connection, they had been broken.

George Orwell was not a prole. He was sympathetic to their pain and even preferred to live amongst them, but he was not one of them.

A rapper is ridiculed for claiming the difficulties of the street life when they grew up in the suburbs with a fully packed lunch made by their mothers and fathers that would whoop them for being out past dark. That's what happens when the middle class tries to relate to the proles. The proles were a most special class though, and Crystal-Dawn was quite proudly truly a prole with the typical prole dream of equality. Not all proles dreamed of winning the lottery and becoming the upper class. They just wanted to live without fear. It was not fear of death, for death was the rest offered at the end of a long arduous journey. The journey was torturous. If a species existed in our world with a suicide rate similar to the human race, we would consider them to have the intelligence of Lemmings. Humans have a great intellect though, so it is difficult for someone who does not have suicidal thoughts to grasp why or how someone could do such a thing. Natural treatments were becoming available with the use of psilocybin to reduce suicidal tendencies in individuals who were not having a temporary crisis, but there is a long reoccurring battle with depression and suicidal thoughts. Such treatments were only recently becoming legal as mushrooms with psychedelic properties had been targeted as dangerous and made illegal for half a century.

Gerrasimos and Crystal-Dawn had recently been on a spiritual journey to Dunn Lake. Her personal realizations were aided by two heroes' doses of psilocybin. She had tried mushrooms before in small enough doses to make the lights a little more brilliant and even made the patterns in the rock faces of the great mountains dance but never anything more. Let me share with you the experiences of a real, first-time trip for the purposes of trying to "reset".

1. Quit smoking.
2. Remove suicidal thoughts.

Begin a new healthy journey of good eating habits and connecting with each other.

Here's the notes translated and recorded from the journal of Gerrasimos and Crystal-Dawn's amazing adventures. Photos are provided; however, the art of cursive handwriting is being lost among the future generations, so a clear translation is provided.

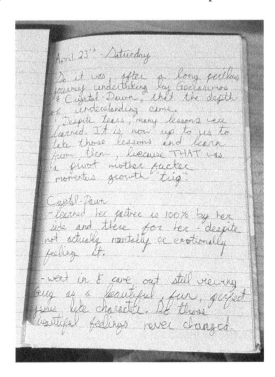

"April 23, Saturday

So it was after a long perilous journey undertaking by Gerrasimos and Crystal-Dawn, that the depth of understanding came. Despite tears, many lessons were learned. It is now up to us to take those lessons and learn from them, because THAT was a pivot motherfucker momentus "trip".

Crystal-Dawn

- learned her partner is 100% by her side and there for her despite not actually mentally or emotionally feeling it.
- went in & came out still viewing Gerry as a beautiful, fun, perfect, Jesus-like character. So beautiful feelings never changed.
- learned our whole world is connected in a way never previously seen although always knew existed.
- learned that others too have seen this and either:

    1. become activists—teach others
    2. become gurus—peaceful & inclusive—not actively seeking change but demonstrating in their own peaceful existence
    3. remain unchanged—not learning lessons
    4. losing hope for mankind because something so beautiful exists in our world and yet negativity & disconnectedness reigns. They leave their hopeful self in that beautiful world & return to the rat race
    5. were the worst negative to begin with & are afraid of what they see. They don't see the beauty of the connectedness

Myself

- I learned I love my natural self & I pity women who don't love or even know what their natural self look like.

- I learned I don't want to do anything without Gerry. doesn't matter how good it is, without him, I don't want it.
- I learned I am too easily swayed in my emotions and it's too much for Gerry.
- That means a serious step-up pivot motherfucker now and gain emotional control of your thoughts.
- Hugging old trees is healing & connecting.
- Talking to nature is good. It answers. It heals.
- Nature is all connected in a beautiful lit web of life
- There is no magic answer or cure or thing you can do to instantly be better—it's just realizing what's really happening and making the choice to do better and be better.
- I had already decided my family comes first—what does this mean? Be their emotional support. Gerry's got the physical stuff—your job is emotional & physical healing. Schedule daily time to talk & physically heal—foot rubs, back rubs, scalp rubs, etc.

- MAKE TIME FOR YOURSELF FOR THE LOVE OF GOD (you). You need to think & heal too & poisoning yourself does not do that. I am killing myself, physically & mentally by smoking, and it is not ok. It is gross. You need to speak up for yourself even to yourself and say NO. I need to heal from the negativity thrust upon me. They won't let me fix, to the poison I fill myself with. No more negative poison."

Would you believe after typing all that, she got up to have a cigarette break outside? Really and truly. These were just words until they were acted upon. It did help reinforce the thought by reading it though. She could feel the pain deep in her throat. Her lungs typically wheezed as they were almost constantly lined with mucus. It was asthma, but truly when one backed away from the small health issues to the big picture, it was inflammation. Inflammation was what happened when the body attacks itself trying to heal you. Our world is on fire. We are in an extreme state of emergency—globally. There is good cause for the anxiety we all feel. Yet we dull our body's alarms with pharmaceuticals, alcohol, distractions, and entertainment. Lupus is an example of inflammation where the body is randomly attacking itself. Like a guard that has been blinded yet still wielding a sword in defense, your immune system is attacking a problem, and you're not listening to what the problem is. If your mind is shutting off your body's signals, your body acts blindly and attacks itself instead of the real problem.

Chapter 1

Throughout time, animalkind has proven its unique ability to adapt and diversify. Whether it was the cooking of meat or the eating of fungi is unknown, but a change occurred that boosted animalkind above all other living things on earth. This change was intellect. Animals did not have the strength of a mighty oak to withstand the elements. A hierarchy developed that was shown in the Great Pyramids. It was a guide to rule animalkind. The animals claimed mysterious secrets of the pyramids, both in the seemingly unattainable perfection of their design but also lack of technology for the time. Few failed to see the big picture of what the pyramids taught animalkind. Some knew the secrets though. They hid them away within a mighty machine.

It was on Manor Farm in England that a plan was created by both man and pigs. Just as capitalists and Communists claim to be of opposing beliefs, so too the pigs and men came together for the common purpose of enslaving animalkind. Once they got past the petty disputes where the borders would lie, they created a device so devious it would be an animal-fueled power machine. The pigs were lower in evolution than man and still envied the materialism and money that man seemed to possess. The men recognized the pigs as a necessary tool as they had proven upon inspection of the farm to be able to create higher production without upgrading life for the workers. It was their greed that created the machine. Men had a secret hidden in their possession that they made known to the pigs. Knowledge of its existence had been rumored throughout history, but it was only now revealed what the Ark of the Covenant was. Mankind had dug so deeply into the earth they had uncovered the earth's heart.

It started with a journey in search of the fountain of youth. It had long ago been discovered the fountain of youth was WATER, straight up pure WATER. The animals' bodies were made of it and needed it to thrive because they too had once come from the water. The men quickly poisoned the animals' water supply. Then they dammed the springs from the fountain of youth to create more POWER! They provided a little power to the animals at an inflated, ever-growing toll that chained them to the machine. The animals needed power for the new world that was being created for them. They needed to work to earn money to pay for a little power. Some animals limited their families' power use by restricting bathing times and cleaning of clothing. Sanitary needs were not met because the cost of power was so high. Some animals didn't have any power at all. They didn't know it, but they were the lucky ones. The grumbling in their stomachs did not make them feel fortunate though as they ate handfuls of dirt, washed down by poisoned water to settle the pain that made sleep impossible.

The animals could block out the hunger pangs during the day while they worked, but when the body was allowed to fall into a state of rest, it demanded to be fed. Sleep was nearly impossible.

The men had long known how to control animals with the basic necessities of life—food, water, and shelter. Space used to exist on this list, but it was discovered the animals were not only willing to cram themselves into the smallest space possible, but they would enslave themselves in debt and create bidding wars for its purchase. Ah yes, shelter, it was such an easy tool to manipulate. They stacked the animals in little crates hundreds of stories high, stacked upon each other. Men had long ago learned the art to enslave animalkind in so many forms. What they failed to do was break some of the animals of their hope. Surely if this machine was run autonomously, fueled by the energy of the animals to create power for man, they had to break the hope some animals held, or surely it would lead to another revolution just as Manor Farm had fallen to. Man learned from history, and although Mr. Jones, the original owner of Manor Farm, was weak and allowed this revolution, it offered many lessons to be learned from. So too, these pigs that sat before them, gambling away their petty means in desperate desire to live the lives of men, could offer them many lessons in how they managed to twist the minds of the animals and kill hope within them.

Men had followed the streams of the fountains of youth and began digging. Surely there must be an even greater treasure within. This was how man came to uncover the earth's heart around approximately AD 1480. At least that was what the trees said. Deep within the mountains where the rivers and streams began, there lay the strong, eternal beating heart of the earth. They had excavated the earth around it and erected mass scaffolding. This was the beginning of the Industrial Revolution. What affected the heart affected the earth and all living things upon it. This capitalist revolution affected the entire earth and spread as blood disease, pumped by the heart to all living parts both within and dependent upon it.

The men had no thought for any species than itself. The taking of life to create the resource of power was without a need for justification.

Who was there above them to justify their actions? Their empire was built like the pyramids with great precision, planning, and on the backs of the animals. What the animals did not know was that men did not plan on staying on the earth. They despised the soil that was Earth's flesh. They leeched it of its nutrients and called it dirt. Dirt was labeled as bad. Men meant to drain the Earth and leave for their manifest destiny in the heavens. They would move from celestial body to celestial body, draining it of all resources to create more fuel to create more POWER. Man's thirst for power was insatiable as they had never mentally evolved past the beginning stages of selfishness. It was within a living being's existence that it grows and experiences, takes and contributes to those around it, then once it had grown to a point of selflessness, it would surrender itself in the ultimate sacrifice back to Earth so that all other living things could benefit from its existence.

Men disagreed with the natural order and wished to break free. They wished to be immortal but recognized the failure of their physical bodies. The same poisons that polluted the earth had so too poisoned their own supply, and they grew weak. At the end of the 1960s man had achieved reaching another celestial body but so far had not extracted any resources other than offering vacation excursions to the animals that could afford it. The machine created by men and pigs was a work of pure engineering genius. It is completely true they hijacked the efforts of visionaries throughout time to either impede or twist their efforts to more self-serving purposes. Outside of the machine, the world had developed into a different place since the original Manor Farm revolution in 1917.

By the twenty-first century, the machine had been running for four centuries and had self-evolved into a device man could not have predicted. They may have been out in the vast expanse of space, immortalized by their own machine, but it was more than likely they had died long ago and their heirs were now much different than themselves. They had evolved to a form other than a restrictive physical form. They were now thoughts, the highest expression of an individual being. Still with no thought for other species, they cared only for themselves and were manifested as negative thoughts. They had learned how to occupy the few centimeters inside the animals' skulls that were their own and exploited it for personal gain. Once again, a device was developed by a visionary that could be used to connect all animals globally. However, all devices allowed in existence were to be for the self-serving purposes of exploiting the animals for power. This Potentially Dangerous Device (PDD) was permitted under great review when it was learned animalkind would prefer to look at images of the young of lesser species. It was fascinating the relationship animalkind had developed with the lesser species.

Animals themselves had evolved, dispersed, and diversified. The natural migration of animals couldn't be stopped, but it could be controlled. Who was to exercise the control required to run the machine? Does every great machine not need operators or a mechanic? The heart was already showing signs of weakness in the 1930s when the machine experienced a surge of power in the twenties from mass production. The Earth reflected this weakness by not producing food to sustain the animals. Other species suffered too of course, but the machine had taught the animals to think like men and be selfish, not selfless. They persuaded the animals with luxuries, higher rewards for those who rose above others of course. The animals could not rise unless it was on the back of another. The heart needed repair and the machine did not allow for shutdowns outside of the mandated yearly one-week shutdown. In this week, the machine would run off an auxiliary source of energy, so trade animals could be brought in for repairs and cleaning. The machine produced too much waste and was an incredible fire hazard for the amount of heat energy being produced by the heart. The shutdown was a necessity of its existence. Trade animals were low enough in the pyramid of society to not be a risk for seeing the heart and telling of its existence. The majority could be bought off for their time as they were willing to sell weeks of their life at a time 24/7 for what they thought was a lot of money. The ones that had a conscience and would tell could easily be disposed of. Physical enforcers were needed for the machine since the thoughts that man had become could not do the tasks required of a physical being. The cats, ever somewhat loyal, while also somewhat dominating man, were the enforcers.

The cats had diversified to such a great extent that they now ranged from a house cat to a lion. No great animals were allowed to be in existence as they were difficult to control. The elephants were hunted to near extinction and would soon be remembered as the great dinosaurs once were. A species too large to be sustained by the resources of the Earth. The truth was the elephants, being the large- of statured creatures that they are, were not only whistleblowers, but their triumphant trumpet could also start an uncontrollable stampede. The destruction of the stampede was encouraged; however, it was the unreliability of being unable to control the elephants that made them undesirable for the machine. Some elephants were allowed to start stampedes intentionally, but that was only the sick ones that the thoughts had impregnated with hate. They could be controlled. The smaller animals were fine though. The more they shouted, their voices were added to an inaudible, indistinguishable sound of madness.

The cats were apex predators. Being on top of the pyramid, they killed any and all they were so capable of killing. They preferred to prey on birds. Birds were a special species. As they diversified, so many species emerged, yet they were all still birds! Birds were typically viewed as undesirable as they created a lot of noise. While many songbirds still sang beautiful songs that filled the world with hope, they were still sometimes viewed as an annoyance and a particular treat to cats. The flamboyant flamingos and stoic peacocks were greatly admired and revered by many animals. It was publicly known the flamingos got their flamboyancy from the money of their followers, and the peacocks had a terrible temper and would charge and attack without warning. Sometimes it was just a warning. It had recently been exposed that the crows had hidden so many shiny objects they were capable of ending world hunger many times over. What made the birds special was that they held the power of hope. In their songs, if they chose to share their words, were inspirational messages of hope that could both encourage, inspire, and enslave all animals.

Remember, only that which feeds the machine and works in accordance with it will be allowed. Hope was necessary in small amounts as without it all animals would choose to perish because the power of thought allowed for the reality of the world to be seen for what it truly was. The Earth herself maintained her beauty on the surface in some places, but in others, it was so terribly scarred. Her natural beauty was what still gave most animals hope daily. They could see the machine was breaking and grew afraid the more they learned the truth of what would happen to the machine at its current and increasing rate of production.

Animals cared, most of them. Some of them? Most definitely some of them, but their voices were washed out by the barking of dogs. Dogs loved the attention! They could be all variants from cautious, fierce, and mistrusting to kind, loving, and loyal. What motivates dogs is unknown as they don't typically speak words worth value. They bark a lot, loudly. Sometimes of value to alert for real danger but typically just make noise that makes it difficult to think a complete thought of value. Many animals had other animals as pets as they preferred a more "taken care of" approach to life. They were typically loving to their owners and listened, but that became rarer and required special training. A naturally loyal companion was almost unheard of, but those companions are always remembered. The others typically destroyed their own environment and sought a means of escape from what they did not know. They just wanted to go run and meet other dogs and do what dogs do. The wolves were a fiercer variety than the domesticated dog. They did not bark at the wind. They howled at the other celestial body, the moon in hopes man was out there and would come back for him. Though wild, a wolf would always be led to the campfire in search of food. Wolves are predators too, don't you know? They are beautiful, mysterious, ferocious yet loving to their own kind. Most wolves run in packs and take victims down together as a group. They typically meet in colleges and universities these days in fraternities but sometimes as young as high school. The wolves were tolerated apex predators due to the machine's ability to control with Ffood as their bodies require a high energy supply, supplied only by the machine. Some lone wolves do exist, but it is seldom you see a wolf make a friend of another species.

On that day at Manor Farm when the men and pigs had sat drinking and fighting over the simultaneous use of the ace of spades between Napoleon and Mr. Pilkington, no one noticed in the uproar a dragonfly sat silently on the wall. It sat for long periods in complete stillness, taking in all around it then switched to great action and flight. It held the power of hope but not in its song as with the birds as no one understood the frequency at which the dragonfly spoke. It surely had thoughts of its own. Not many knew how long a dragonfly lived because they always died in captivity or lived and existed in some unknown imaginary world of magic. They gave animals hope at the sight of them. Imagine having the power to incite hope by just being yourself. That was the true power of an individual. The machine knew by the eventual, all-earth-consuming goal of consuming resources for power, ecosystems and habitats would eventually all be destroyed. Wherever the "magical" place was the dragonflies came from would be found, and all dragonflies would cease to exist. They were generally tolerated though and seen as a pest than a fire starter.

This dragonfly listened intently to the plan to build the machine and how it would run. It was the most painful absorption of horrible, deplorable words illustrating how animals would be used as fuel for the machine. They weren't just using their dead physical bodies for fuel anymore as they once had done sending Boxer the cart horse to market for slaughter for glue. They were taking the animals very time on Earth, their life existence, and soaking every moment possible to fuel the machine with their energy. Not only would they do it willingly, but they would LOVE it. They would LOVE the exchange because the machine would create so many personal problems within the home and self. There would be no other choice of how one would choose to spend their time. Most animals had poor vision due to the use of potentially dangerous devices (PDD). These PDDs could be amazing tools but overuse damaged the user. That was the doubled-edged sword of technology made possible by the machine. How could a tool that could connect all animals be allowed to exist if it was not also used for the machine's purposes?

The tool was an interface for the machine. The machine could now directly infiltrate the animals' minds and do everything. It could plant seeds you see. This seeder could be used to plant good seeds of knowledge and truth. It could hold all the collective history and knowledge of the world into the future. It was a great sword that cast the illusion of being wielded by some and none simultaneously. Few animals even understood it. They just really enjoyed it! Due to being the interface of a machine, it had an online world where animals could be whoever they wanted to be. THIS was an illusion of power and in fact enslaved the animals to an *Alice in Wonderland* world of controlled reality, constantly for sale to the highest bidder. The very souls and presence of the animals online made capital for the machine. The capital was just another word for money, the thing the animals were forced to trade their lives for. Once again, the PDDs were a dream and a curse. It freed those chained by their geographical, financial, social, and physical restrictions and real-life implications.

So seldom were online issues resolved in the real world as there were enough problems in the real world created by the machine, the animals preferred using their PDDs for entertainment and distraction than to hear about the problems created by the machine in the real world. The PDDs had made it clear the life the animals knew and enjoyed was nearing its end. They didn't want to think about it. It had been learned throughout time; it shortens the life living in distress. Rather than fix the distressing problem, it was easier to believe the thoughts of man that there was no real hope or anything animals could do to fix the machine.

It had grown far beyond that of any one of the animals' understanding. No one wanted the Earth to die as all species were dependent upon it. The machine had been set up by man, not even one man but many, many pigs and men. With the division of entropy being the eventual doom of the machine, the animals' division of labor was now specialized occupations, thoroughly understanding all parts under a microscope but being unable to see the picture as a whole. From their microscopes, the future was doomed. Whether it be by war, natural disaster, atomic disaster, biological, or even cosmic means, life the way animals knew it would cease. They had been born into the machine and never knew of anything different so how were they to know or dream of having the power to fix the machine before it killed the Earth and all the species on it.

The doves recognized the dragonfly as a symbol of change, transformation, and self-realization. It teaches us to love life and to rejoice and have faith even amid difficulties. They recognized the great presence of this dragonfly as significant. Throughout time, the energy that is within this dragonfly has resurfaced in many forms to tell the other animals of the knowledge it possesses. The knowledge of this machine, how and why it was made, and how to fix it. You would think each time a dragonfly appears throughout time, the animals would stand in awe, but they did not. Some of the animals printed pictures and made statues of its shape, but few thought that specific energy existed in all dragonflies. The energy came as an elephant sometimes, loudly warning the other animals. He was quickly killed for the value of its ivory. Sometimes the energy came back as a variety of birds, but the cats were shrewd, and it had been tried many times. It typically ended in an excruciating demise. After so many lives and deaths, experiences, and growth of thought, it began to transform under the great pressures put upon it. The very fires that once burned the so-called heretic applied so much heat and pressure, that one dragonfly's energy rose from the ashes like a phoenix. This time it radiated so much energy it could barely be contained in a physical form. It became something that appeared different to all that looked upon it. While still maintaining one physical form in each animal's perceived reality, it looked different. You may envision a phoenix, but in fact, the great pressure applied to this carbon life force created a crystal. This crystal was incredibly reflective, not like that of a mirror that shows you, you, but that which reflected something different. Whether it was its own unique life force or merely the energy absorbed from everything around it was unclear.

Some saw a mother duck surrounded by obedient ducklings that stayed in line for the most part.

Some saw a mother cougar standing guard over her young, awaiting danger.

Some saw a strong workhorse, whether they recognized the intellect of being able to complete a task was up to the individual.

Some saw an enemy..

That was the problem with the world. The animals thought the twenty-first century was boring and nothing of interest happened, but that was merely because they did not see that which they were immersed in. It was in the twenty-first century that the final dividing blow of individualism influenced a generation to create the change that was needed to make it the final blow.

The last generations had great confusion to deal with as they were being told to think for themselves while being told what to think while simultaneously not knowing what to think or even wanting to think. It would be amusing or even a humorous satire; however, these were real people. Young people were real people too. They were just being shaped by the reality of the machine. The machine told them they could be anything they wanted to be if they worked really, really hard or not because they shouldn't have to do anything they don't want to. Life was full of these extreme contradictions, the dividers of animalkind. The world was so confused. Animals were being born into the wrong gender bodies.

11:00 p.m.

Crystal-Dawn stops typing and closes the computer. Gerrasimos was done in the bath and headed to bed. That was the place to be right now next to that warm Greek chiseled statue body of a man.

May 7, 2022

Like clockwork Crystal-Dawn sprung from the bed. It was a lot better to get the coffee started than to lay there with thoughts that were beginning to redirect her mood negatively. That was no way to start the day. Granted, there was reason to feel sad. It was a Saturday and most weekends this would mean Gerrasimos rising from bed early to wake his daughter for dance class. After they left, Crystal would wait for his son to rise to get him breakfast. Those kids too had an internal alarm like clockwork. This was now the second weekend in a row they were not being allowed visitation. This time the excuse was that it was Mother's Day weekend. They had asked for one night and were told no. Next weekend she also had plans with them out of town, and while she never directly said, "I'm keeping them," she merely vaguely stated she was booking a hotel in another town for their daughter's competition, so it was assumed she wanted them with her. An email had been sent asking for more communication and clarity. Also, if weekends could be a more scheduled visitation that was maintained rather than changed every weekend. Her response was to say it was hurtful and demeaning and would be keeping the children. Her family had houseboats and ski cabins, BMWs, and political offices. When their lawyers refused to follow the law, Gerrasimos had been left with nothing in their separation, not even a written agreement protecting his visitation rights.

Do you see how this is the petty type of dispute that keeps individuals from rising to the challenge of helping the whole world? How is one supposed to help others when they can't even see their own children for weeks at a time? Does one merely admit defeat and skip on with their day, or does one resist and cause battles? They say, "Pick your battles."

Funny enough, for a woman who had received so many death threats over the years, Crystal-Dawn had no enemies. How was this possible? It is best explained as an insult. You see an insult is not an insult unless the person being insulted FEELS insulted. If the person does not feel insulted by the words, then no insult has been made; words have merely been spoken to which the listener awards no meaning. If an ant one day told a human that the human was despicable, would the human feel offended at the words of such a tiny ant? It's hard to imagine beyond the shock of a speaking ant, but you get the idea.

Many people thought they didn't like Crystal. Her old boss, someone that had helped her over the years and had been a mentor and friend, would also remind her that three people could keep a secret if two of them were dead. He used to be like a grandfather to her, and she would gather the stories of his life as they spent days driving in the sun checking traps. They spent a lot of time in the graveyard. He wanted a memorial with a screen in it that people could press play, and it would show a video of his life. He had an amazing life and Crystal-Dawn wanted to be just like him, not exactly of course. He had been a golf pro at that time. He said she would need full-time employment to pay the bills if she wanted to eventually be a full-time trapper with a trapline. That was why Crystal signed up to be a plumber. It had the lowest math prerequisite, and she had welded as a child, so brazing and soldering sounded enjoyable. It also offered an opportunity to bring clean water and wastewater treatment facilities to communities in need globally.

Even though she had heard directly from new clients that her old boss had warned them to not give her business, she still considered him an old friend and mentor. She was the first to visit him and his wife with flowers after Covid restrictions ended. He had been kind and warm and told her stories of his recent brain surgery, and she was the first person he had seen aside from his immediate family in a long time. Despite their history, Crystal has no enemies, just an understanding of why. That's all you need sometimes is to know why.

Gerrasimos left to play a game of "golf" on the pool table. They had forgotten about the meeting with the president of the Army Navy and were going to need to do something because the men would ask what news Gerrasimos had. Crystal would need to write a proper email. Sometimes you need to gather all the information before beginning something though. Crystal wanted to create something amazing for her partner and all these friends that just wanted other friends to talk to and play with. Gerrasimos had a passion for pool but had been made to feel guilty for it in the past. Crystal recognized it to be a natural source of dopamine for him and encouraged him to get out and spend time on himself. She even developed a lucky charm for his success of the day.

Crystal-Dawn could get lost in thought for hours thinking about Gerrasimos but now was time for writing her book. He would be gone for a few hours. One child was on a sleepover, one had not woken up, and the other was doing homework. It was a great time to get some uninterrupted writing done.

Today was a momentous day in history. Remember Crystal-Dawn viewed her own personal life as having all the same experiences and problems of the world? Today a great thing had occurred. Two great superpowers came together. One had initiated it and suggested peace! This superpower had been like Russia or China, completely sealed off from the rest of the family. Crystal had approached him once at Christmas time. She planted a seed. That seed was love, family, understanding, and respect. She had some negative reactions to it of course as many didn't want people to connect. They want people to feel as alone as they feel, so they dragged them away from family and locked them away in their own hateful reality of the world. It was hard for people to break away from.

This mention of a peace talk stirred a lot of feelings! The most peaceful of all the superpowers was the one that surprisingly came out with guns blazing! Crystal-Dawn told her so. She tried to calm the superpower and helped her see why the other superpower had not the nerve to contact her directly. She had her dukes up. No different than when an individual explains an injustice with an uproar of negative energy, she too was holding this pent-up energy from the past. Of course, she had every right to. Wrongs had been committed. Were they to simply be forgotten and not addressed? The pain and suffering that superpower had brought to their mother was so great how could it ever be forgiven? It would never be forgotten in her mind. The third superpower, and perhaps the most typically explosive of all, was surprisingly hesitant and unknowing what to do, granted this was thirdhand information at this point and would only be known when the big meeting occurred.

Crystal-Dawn begged to be present. She was told twice that this did not include her. All three superpowers were definitely needing to meet together, and unless Crystal could be there as a helpful, healing Crystal, absorbing the negative energy, and radiating it out as a positive rainbow of peace, she feared the meeting may not go as splendidly as it once could have.

Gerrasimos and Crystal-Dawn had their own dreams for the land. Gerrasimos wanted to build self-sustainable farms in repurposed storage

containers that could be shipped to communities globally. Crystal-Dawn wanted to renovate his grandmother's house, restoring it to the beautiful yet simple homestead it had once been when they were the first pioneers of Lumby Valley. His grandmother and grandfather had run a farm and developed a trailer park for thousands of individuals who called it home for decades. He had a logging company too!

His grandmother once wrote a poem.

> My Lover was a Logger,
> stirred his coffee with his thumb
> Saturday night 'twas the Legion.
> With his nose in a bottle of rum.
> Come Sunday morn you'd find him,
> With his head between his knees,
> Askin', "Lord will ya, take this headache please."
> ...

There was more but the handwriting was not always the easiest to translate.

Regardless, they were amazing people that worked hard and contributed to creating the community. Crystal-Dawn dreamed that the city of Lumby would be interested in purchasing the farm one day and would run it as a historic site with park and river access for the local trailer park residents and also offer over sixty acres of farmable land for any purposes that could create revenue to pay off the purchase of the land. It seemed like a beautiful plan that would benefit all superpowers simultaneously. Crystal could create gardens in the memory of the grandfather and the grandmother though she was still alive and in a home, so wouldn't it be amazing if the superpowers could find PEACE while she was still alive? So she could see the beautiful things that had been done with her land and look back on her memories with pride as time well spent and not lost on financial greed, swallowed up by yet another multimillionaire investor from the coast. All the land was getting swallowed up, and those investors did not care to preserve the memories of those who cleared the land before them or the lessons they learned from the land while clearing it.

There was hope.

Hope Lies with the Proles

Crystal-Dawn resumed writing *Animal Farm Part II* feverishly now. It had to be written. These words needed to be heard.

Chapter 2

The crystal was unique in every way while still bearing the properties unique to a crystal. A crystal is defined as a piece of a homogeneous solid substance having a natural geometrically regular form with symmetrically arranged plane faces. Also, it was a highly transparent glass with a high refractive index. Crystals vibrate to many frequencies at once. Health is the natural state of any form in the universe. Considering the vibrational existence of reality health comes with, frequencies of anything are in harmony and balance itself. When patterns of energy are disrupted, we experience a state which we know as disease, which is a body that is not at ease. The resistant, discordant energy patterning is responsible for every negative symptom the animals experience.

Crystals have a vibration that is free of resistant patterns. They are among some of the structures in the physical dimension which have the most balanced, cohesive, strong, and intentional frequencies. Their unchanging physical structure is a reflection of their innate energetic pattern of balance and strength which are incorruptible.

This crystal carried the story of the machine. It absorbed the energy of the past. Some thoughts long forgotten were alive within this crystal, it had the power to heal, strengthen, encourage, inspire, and radiate. It could even resurrect the dead. Men wanted the crystal for themselves. However, their dark energy was radiated by the crystal, and they did not like what they saw. It was an unbearable energy to those who were not meant to have it. The crystal needed to be refilled with loving energy.

When left alone, it absorbed the energy of the sun and walked barefoot upon the Earth's body.

It wanted to be a rainbow, but that was not what it was. It was not the crystal that made animals hopeful. It was the positive energy radiated by the crystal, the visible rainbow. Just because it was intangible and could not be held or captured, it did not mean it was an illusion. It was real. It was something that showed the animals the true presence of the colors of the light. Though they could not always see it, it was there—beautiful rainbows filtering all around the animals, filling them with energy. The crystal merely made it possible to see this real world of beauty by being in the right place at the right time, absorbing energy, and radiating it so others could see the rainbow.

The crystal's power was also evident in the rain. Water was the Earth's blood and when the rain got heavy in the skies, it clung to particles of dust, pulling them to the ground. The rain could clear the dustiest of skies. With the machine's production increasing, the skies fell dark with haze.

The animals did not even see it for themselves unless they traveled far away from the machine. The air made it hard for the animals to see much further than the ends of their own noses sometimes! The ones who had found the fresh air and were able to see the blue skies above the clouds tried telling the other animals to open their eyes. It was quite painful to do so as the poison in the air burned their eyes.

The Earth needed the machine to keep its heart running now, and all animalkind's existence was dependent on the heart's continued beating. Only some knew of the heart's existence, and those who did had no interest in accepting to fix it. Those animals were comfortable in their jobs.

The crystal knew how to fix it, and once again, this lifetime around continued to radiate the hope for animalkind. It eventually met its twin flame. Hiding in an abandoned glass plant was a very special energy. His flame had been put out to a smoldering ember but was still clearly visible by the crystal. He labored away trying to save the fallen giants of the tree kingdom. These trees had lived their lives to their fullest and were destined to be firewood for the animals to keep warm. He saved them from the fires and cared for them. He was a collector of the stories of the forest. His light shone through the trees, and his ember was about to ignite from all the wood shavings that filled his shop. He was of the merman evolutionary line. He had transcended far beyond that of a mere fish and man and was just needing a little radiated heat energy to ignite. Together they were unstoppable.

The purpose of the machine was to instill division among the animals. As long as the crystal and merman were together, they proved the loving bond between individuals was stronger than the machine. No matter how they disagreed at times or how often the merman refused to want to see the positivity of the crystal, he eventually gave himself over to its healing powers. It took a long time to regain his trust though as it would with most of animalkind. Together they had the power to change the world. His intellect and its emotional strength were enough to convince all the animals. But would they listen this time? The crystal had tried again and again throughout time. Were the animals ready to save the heart of the Earth? Would they even gather to listen to what it would take before deciding it could not be done?

May 8, 2022
Mother's Day

Crystal-Dawn's children were a loving explosion of kindness to wake to. The youngest, in her usual, overachieving loving way, made a large breakfast for everyone and walked to get a fresh extra-large, triple-triple coffee. Something happened on this walk as it tended to happen a lot these days. A very special book fell from someone's vehicle onto the road. It was run over a few times, but she fetched it. This book was exactly what Crystal had been asking for, an understanding of the indigenous peoples of Canada! She had asked to meet many, many times over the years with the local leaders and elders. She even once walked straight into a band office without an appointment and exploded to the first person she saw that she was trying to help the world, and no one would talk with her. The man had been extremely kind but was unsure how he could be of assistance as he oversaw housing. Crystal had tried befriending an indigenous woman in a store but had never received a response. Her two old friends from college were both busy in their own lives as well. The only indigenous person Crystal knew was an old trapper she had done some work for once. He gave great insight as to what it was like being a member of the band. While he had been incredibly helpful in providing contact information for the band chiefs, he had a personal vendetta with politics, and it was difficult to direct these thoughts away from the injustices he had experienced. Crystal-Dawn once knew an indigenous woman in Merritt when she was a child. She had been friends with the woman's children. Her name was Andrea and she had three young children. She had told stories of working hard to not live on the reserve. She had a good office job and provided a nice home for her kids. She had a beautiful light in her that shone in her smile. One morning her kids tried to wake her, but she would not wake up. She died in her early thirties from an aneurysm. Her children went to live with family on the reserve. As a taxidermist, Crystal had met many indigenous people wanting to sell animals or looking to have work done. It was always a confusing area of the law and typically one that was better avoided. Even the conservation officers could not provide a straight answer as to what the laws were with indigenous people and their possession and use of wildlife.

Can you imagine a young white woman having to tell a grown native man the government says he can't have that eagle without a permit from them. Therefore, she could not do the work for him because she couldn't take it without a permit or she would be charged. There was outrage not at Crystal of course but at the system. She absorbed many rantings by many people over the course of her life. Thankfully Gerrasimos was deeply engaged with the new book their daughter had brought home so he would be able to give Crystal highlights while she wrote throughout the day.

This unfortunately became a twisted conversation where Crystal sulked off with hurt in her heart. This happened quite frequently and could be easily disregarded but was typically still a reoccurring issue that did cut her deeply. Her partner had been reading and had questions on how an indigenous society would thrive if the leaders that rose were not elders with beliefs rooted in culture but rather the capitalist's beliefs to grow their communities economically. The problem was it felt as though every time someone told Crystal they didn't understand something, she would try to explain. She wouldn't get a full sentence out half the time before being told, "No no, not like that. Like this." This was incredibly frustrating because when people spoke, they didn't learn. They already knew that information. Then someone presents new information and without even trying to gain an understanding of what information is being presented, it is already dismissed.

That was how Crystal felt at her lowest, dismissed, unworthy, disregarded, not worth hearing the thoughts, and not worth getting to know. It was the tune that rang throughout her whole life. There may have been some who stood out over time as truly having loved her and cared for her, but she always pondered, *How can you love something without getting to know it? If you did love something, would you not want to know everything about it and marvel at its magnificence?* That kind of love was deemed to not exist anymore. To even speak of it was to suggest that one person live entirely for the other as their main priority and purpose in life. How dare one suggest such chains on another!

They were not meant to be chains, but some people saw them as such, having experienced the bondage and lashings firsthand. Have you considered that? When a partner is subjected to verbal abuse, it is no different from being chained in your home every day after work and taking a verbal lashing. Some wounds went deep too. People did not consider the power of words anymore. If something was of a reason to cause suspicion, it was now—sus. That's it. People hurled the most hateful and hurtful of words and expected that the other person, a family member, friend, or coworker just forget it and pretend it never occurred. It was one of the most common, daily forms of brainwashing people did to each other and themselves. They said they were joking; they didn't mean it, oversensitive or too emotional. It became so commonplace to say hateful things that even the leader of Canada Justin Trudeau stated that the unvaccinated were misogynists

Evolved Individual, that could rise above the petty stresses that weighed down all, but particularly the proles. This was a gift of balance Crystal had made for her children and made available to the world.

It originally started as a balance pie chart she made while studying psychology for herself. Crystal suffered from a lack of balance, being the extremist she was. I do believe unless someone puts great personal effort into being balanced, we are all naturally unbalanced. We seek that which we need in all the wrong ways.

We need connection and approval from our peers, so we turn on our devices and feel the instant gratification of acceptance from someone halfway around the world while ignoring the very neighbors that sit beside us on the bus or in the store.

We need to feel attractive, so we find the right angle and filter and love only that view of ourselves rather than work on the inner joy that makes our smiles radiate, exposing the truest and most beautiful version of ourselves!

We decide we don't like something before becoming fully informed and turn that dislike into a dislike for the person and not the thing we ignorantly decided we don't like. People disconnect from the people around them.

Personal effort will be required on your part and the only person who can do it is you. The majority of this is time for self-reflection. Yes, I'm asking for your time please, but I'm directing your thoughts.

Find a peaceful quiet place.

I like flowing water because it helps my mind not get stuck on thoughts that aren't productive or on topic. Just imagine those thoughts being on a leaf in the water and just flowing away. It might come back a few times but no matter what, the water keeps flowing. Find your quiet place to reflect though. This is about you.

Basic Categories of LIFE

Credit is due to Maslow and other awesome psychologists working to help us understand ourselves better.

and racists, making them enemies of the state. Crystal-Dawn
family were unvaccinated. She most definitely was not a misogy
had been previously engaged to an African man. There was nc
in her blood. There also was no substance in her blood, enforce
much of the world. There were few people remaining that had th
blood. In every scientific experiment, there is always the control
that does not get tested. How else would you be able to get prope
from the effects of the study?

There was something about the blood. It hadn't happened yet,
the stage was ripe for a most terrible occurrence. It was not fores
by some spiritual guidance but rather scientific logic with a touch
personal experience. Jehovah's Witnesses were somewhat known
their stance against blood transfusions. There were recorded cases whe
a Jehovah's Witness child had been forced a transfusion by either a judg
or doctor and the child either died or was handicapped for life. Thes
were true stories. Not all blood transfusions saved lives. Crystal's father
had been a strong believer though, and one of his greatest sacrifices
to mankind, or at least Canadians, was to live a "clean"—drug- and
tattoo-free life, so he could donate blood regularly. In total his sacrifice
could have saved 503 Canadians. That was how many people now
were a part of Crystal's family through blood. She was never able to
be proud of him for this of course. Did you know now with the great
Covid in 2022 in Canada, Canadian Blood Services is accepting blood
from any vaccinated individuals within any time frame of having been
vaccinated without any record being made as to which type of vaccine
is in the blood. Bag upon bags of blood that would have previously had
a strict policy for donations was now not even recording data that could
potentially be life-threatening, potentially because as was the problem
with the rushed vaccine cures, there hadn't been time for the testing to
occur. Would they have really taken the time also to know the long-term
effects of transfusing blood between individuals with different vaccines?

This was an unknown variable and the world was busy with
problems, avoiding problems, entertainment, life stress, work, health,
and finances, all of those were in Crystal's pie chart made from Maslow's
studies. These things all required energy in an individual's life, to be an

Responsibilities

Basic responsibilities as a person are carried by all. Beyond the basics are up to you with how much you can divide your time to be balanced and still manage.

Basic—manage all aspects of your basic responsibilities before adding to this list.

Additional responsibility examples but not limited to

- pets
- vehicle
- owning versus renting a home
- college/university(?)
  - student loans?

They are all your choices to be made in life at any point. Jump in at any age and grab the reins of responsibility in your life. The stress relief will make you a happier person and extend your life.

Employment

As a teenager in British Columbia, employment is optional as we believe you should be focused on your education. However, there is a mandatory minimum of thirty hours of paid career preparation or volunteer community service as a graduation requirement for all BC secondary school students.

Whether paid or volunteer, work experience is a necessity as your resume will be your personal identification for finding employment throughout life.

As independent adults, the majority of us have realized employment is a necessity as without work there's no money, and without that, you are hungry and homeless with HUGE life consequences.

Remember, earning money is not having money as the majority of people in our society including the government is in debt. Don't give it away so easily. That money represents your time, your LIFE. Do your FINANCES!

Finances

Finances are reliant upon employment typically but not in the same category. Hopefully you can always earn an income but that doesn't mean you'll have any money unless you manage it. Be smart! Once again, that money represents your life, and as far as we know, you only get one.

BUDGET

> Taxes
> Saving and budgeting
> Emergency fund
> Bill management
> Retirement
> Managing debts
> Building credit

I am not a financial advisor but they're out there for you to connect with in a way that makes your lifestyle and goals possible

Self-Care

Self-care is of course a requirement, but sometimes we fail to find time for both our inner self and outer self. We can fully admit this category is sometimes out of balance. Women who use makeup and "do" their hair typically spend an hour a day working on their outer selves so the world can see a version of them, but do they take that equal amount of time on their inner selves?

Inner Self

Esteem needs what Maslow classified into two categories: (i) esteem for oneself (dignity, achievement, mastery, independence) and (ii) the need to be accepted and valued by others (e.g., status, prestige).

Self-actualization needs—realizing personal, potential self-fulfillment and seeking personal growth and peak experiences. There is a desire "to become everything one is capable of becoming" (Maslow 1987, p. 64).

Outer Self
Physical Exercise
Nutrition

Aesthetic needs—appreciation and search for beauty, balance, and form

Transcendent needs—a person is motivated by values which transcend beyond the personal self (e.g., mystical experiences and certain experiences with nature, aesthetic experiences, sexual experiences, service to others, the pursuit of science, religious faith, etc.).

It's amazing how much more time your inner self needs than your outer self.

Don't starve yourself. Give your body and mind what they both need.

Friendships

Good friends are wonderful additions to life as they also fill the need for Love and belongingness—friendship, intimacy, trust, and acceptance. These are receiving and giving affection and love and affiliating, being part of a group (family, friends, work).

These are the people who are helping guide you through life, so make sure they're a good influence. You can either be built up by role models or torn down by drama. The choice is yours. This is also the basic building block to finding the love of your life. It has to have a solid foundation of friendship. If you want GOOD friends, then BE a GOOD friend.

If you want to meet a certain kind of person, be the kind of person that person would want to spend time with.

It starts with you.

The only thing in your power is you.

What qualities do you admire?

List them.

Now instead of looking at this list as the potential friend quality list, this is your list of qualities to emulate. Not only will you love yourself, but you will attract like-minded people.

Now that you know who you are, you can start exploring what you like. Go through the activities and try something.

Get CONNECTED with local clubs and organizations!

Get CONNECTED with volunteering in your community.

A very admirable quality is giving of oneself, self-sacrificing, and being helpful.

You'll meet really good people that care about the same things you do and do the same activities you do.

Get CONNECTED.

Family

If you are blessed to have a family that loves you, be grateful! If life automatically selects the cards you are dealt, family is one of those random gambling cards. Whether you come from a good family or would like to start your own one day or are raising the one you currently have, family requires a time commitment. It is one of the most valuable ways to spend your time.

Responsibilities will vary, friends will come and go, and employment and finances will change, but your family is consistently your family throughout your entire life.

Make time to help your parents, no matter your age.

Make time to ask your kids how their day was, no matter your age. Make time for the people you love to grow healthy relationships.

Personal Growth

This is the best category in my opinion. This category also fills the needs of your inner self.

Being well-rounded in life with skills and abilities feels amazing! It's the way you've chosen to develop yourself as a person. Can you speak other languages or have amazing talents? It's because you took the time to learn how. Never stop learning. Never stop growing.

Dreams
Achievements
Skills
Education
Hobbies
Sports
Talents
Contributions to your community
Contributions to the world

Self-sustainability

What does that even mean?

The fate of the human race relies on this, yet it's not often thought of as a common day-to-day goal. How much do you want to drain the planet of its resources and how much do you want to give back?

Educate yourself about self-sustainability and the various innovative projects being done in your community. You too can help make the changes necessary to ensure we leave clean Earth for future generations.

Gardening
Foraging
Cooking

Preserving food
Energy resources
Building/repairing

> A society grows great when old men plant trees
> in whose shade they shall never sit.
> —Greek Proverb

Be the BEST you, you could possibly be!

These were the words written as guidance for Crystal-Dawns children and shared with all mankind. If people could balance these and try them all on a regular basis, they would feel joy and fulfillment.

Would people listen? Would they be filled with faith and hope? Would it move them to action?

May 9, 2022

Make time to ask your kids how their day was, no matter your age. Make time for the people you love to grow healthy relationships.

Personal Growth

This is the best category in my opinion. This category also fills the needs of your inner self.

Being well-rounded in life with skills and abilities feels amazing! It's the way you've chosen to develop yourself as a person. Can you speak other languages or have amazing talents? It's because you took the time to learn how. Never stop learning. Never stop growing.

Dreams
Achievements
Skills
Education
Hobbies
Sports
Talents
Contributions to your community
Contributions to the world

Self-sustainability

What does that even mean?

The fate of the human race relies on this, yet it's not often thought of as a common day-to-day goal. How much do you want to drain the planet of its resources and how much do you want to give back?

Educate yourself about self-sustainability and the various innovative projects being done in your community. You too can help make the changes necessary to ensure we leave clean Earth for future generations.

Gardening
Foraging
Cooking

Preserving food
Energy resources
Building/repairing

> A society grows great when old men plant trees
> in whose shade they shall never sit.
> —Greek Proverb

Be the BEST you, you could possibly be!

These were the words written as guidance for Crystal-Dawns children and shared with all mankind. If people could balance these and try them all on a regular basis, they would feel joy and fulfillment.

Would people listen? Would they be filled with faith and hope? Would it move them to action?

May 9, 2022

Chapter 3

The crystal had called for a meeting of the nations. The animals of the world were divided into three superpowers. The old bears' nation had been sealed off from the rest of the world and little was really known. Their languages were so vastly different than that understood by the others. Communication was rare between them. The old bear was not necessarily bad but had another influence on these thoughts. Remember how men had evolved into a thought? The thoughts of men were greed, all-consuming greed with no end.

"Oranges and Lemons," say the bells of St. Clements.

"You owe me three farthings," say the bells of S. Martens,

"When will you pay me?" say the bells of Old Bailey,

"When I am rich," say the bells of Shoreditch."

This old bear kept his animals locked away as he had been told, not much better than that of the original Manor Farm with Mr. Jones. These were new farms though where Mr. Jones was able to live on a private ranch away from the animals while they worked themselves to death giving energy to the machine so they could get a taste of its power.

How was it going to be possible that an old man of such power would freely relinquish it? The crystal knew. This was why she bore the key for animalkind.

The animals themselves were living in small, cold spaces. Mold, disease, lack of nutritious food, and power made it almost impossible to think about much else. They were told it was overpopulation because they had all moved to these urban centers. These were the cities of sparkling white concrete man had laid out in his dream for animals in the future. It wasn't feasible and created a lack of housing, which in turn caused a great depression in 2020. Youth everywhere began to realize they would never be able to afford their own home and would be doomed to live with their parents forever! The perceived worst fate possible. Parts of this were true as the juveniles of most species typically spread out from their home to find their own like the wolverine or cougar. It is natural for some species. Others grew together in close-knit family groups like meerkats and marmots. Do you notice a distinction? Herbivores were more likely to live together in peaceful groups. The birds flock together, singing their songs of hope all in different notes but all stringing together the most beautiful symphony of nature.

The animals needed to recognize this. How were they to see if there was so much smoke in the cities? Even Africa smelled of fire and smoke so badly it caused one's senses to alarm with fright at DANGER.

Asa, a beautiful African voice rang out to warn the people.

> There is fire on the mountain, and nobody seems to be on the run.
>
> Oh, there is fire on the mountaintop, and no one is a-runnin'.
>
> I wake up in the mornin', tell you what I see on my TV screen
>
> I see the blood of an innocent child, and everybody's watchin'
>
> Now I'm looking out my window, and what do I see?
>
> I see an army of a soldier man marching across the street, yeah

> Hey, Mr. Soldier man, tomorrow is the day you go to war, but you are fighting for another man's cause, and you don't even know him.

("Fire on the Mountain")

Her beautiful words would help at the meeting, but it would not be these words, for she had far more powerful words to say to the great powers of the United Nations. They were the animal jailors, but they were victims too.

The next great power was an explosive, middle-aged wolverine. He would explode at anything! Tale would have it he once threatened a goose who landed on his farm from the sky. As soon as his feet touched that earth, my goodness, that poor goose never knew what he had coming to him. Anyways, he had since realized it was bad for his heart and was trying to be calm. He had once exploded around the crystal. He saw himself reflected in her. He did not like what he saw and immediately changed from anger to calm acceptance. He felt a slight defeat from the way he held his head, but peace was offered at that moment that had changed the entire scenario. She had that power. He never did communicate with her much after that. He knew that she held tales from his past that not even he was aware of mainly because he had never taken the time to ask her. What he saw when he looked at the crystal was his knowledge alone.

The last great power was an elderly horse, not so old as to be feeble as she still cared for her aging mother daily. She was old enough to be tired. She could not rest though as her body ached from previous injuries and made sitting terribly uncomfortable. She was destined to stand or walk the remainder of her days until it was time to rest at night. Like any mother, she spent her life in the loving servitude of others. You wouldn't know she was a horse to look at her physical form as she carried many duties that required many hats to be worn. She might appear as a feeble mouse working away in Cinderella's absence, sewing clothing for the animals, making meals, gardening, and cleaning. The tasks were so great that this woman rose to the heights of a great stallion, carrying her family from here to there in her protection. She was truly selfless. She was at the height of an animal's evolution, but she carried great pains that would not let her rest. Her time was not yet done. She not only carried her own but the pains of others as most mothers did. Great wrongs had been committed to her children—the animals, the land, and the mother. Wanting nothing more than to be at peace in her garden, she had sat by the sidelines and watched the atrocities occur. When it was intolerable, she had tried to exert her power, but she was so tired.

She was an animal too! She was prone to the thoughts of men. With fear and anger, it was mostly the outcry of injustice that she held within that made her real for without it, surely this great power would have been a transcended being not prone to the problems of animals.

Peace talks among these nations had been attempted but never occurred. One was scheduled when the old bear one day approached the wolverine for peace. This meeting had been requested by the crystal previously of course, but the message was never received, lost in the machine. The wolverine's response was surprising. He was hesitant but offered a temporary home as the old bear made clear his intentions of residing on the disputed land, land used by the wolverine but owned by all three powers. Not in equal shares, the bear had taken half, the wolverine and the horse shared the remaining half. Of course, the horse had borne all financial costs while the wolverine took all the profits from revenue earned from the land. It was an unfair situation that would need to be remedied. The grandmother that entrusted them the land did not know of the dealings of the land and did not want to be told of it. She remembered stories of living there and raising her family, but what it was when she left that day for a drive and never returned was a sight she did not want to see. Her land, her farm, and her home had been ruined.

The crystal had a positive intention that could please all the great powers, the animals, and the grandmother. Crystals work that way. You need to set an intention for it to radiate that energy. Did they want peace? Did they want to spread the sting of the hurt of the past, so it could be felt by others too? Was that necessary for healing? An apology most certainly was. An apology for the hurt made and felt by others, for how could one apologize for a hurt they were unaware of a pain they could not understand or perhaps were not even willing to be made aware of?

11:00 p.m.

Crystal-Dawn retired to bed after a long day of writing, working, and being loved as a mother. Every day new revelations were being had that added to the story in such unpredictable ways. You see upon being presented with gifts, Crystal realized how God must feel being presented with gifts from His children. One casually handed her a small bag of granite pebbles she had gathered from a roadside and went on with her day in indifference. The second presented a few spa luxuries she had purchased prior but was in a foul mood throughout the day from other occurrences. The third, as mentioned prior, had gone all out with gifts, the effort for all, and love throughout the day, ending with a long cuddle. As a mother, the observations offered some insight. If there was anything wished for, it would have been that the children show an interest in the activities of their mother. Showed an active interest in the things she had made. After all, she was currently writing a book. Would they not care to hear it, even some of it?

Gerrasimos listened to her. As a father, he could relate. At the end of a long day of productivity, he sat and read a paragraph. He didn't have to, but after spending over twenty minutes trying to convince one child that it would so please her mother if she showed an interest, he gave up and read it himself. It was hard to maintain faith in a future generation that sometimes showed an interest in nothing more than TikTok. The potentially dangerous devices (PDD) were dulling the youth's brains to the extent they literally had no dreams, goals, aspirations, hope, or purpose. Not all fell into this trap, but it was most definitely more than half of the youth in 2022. Who was to blame them? The previous generations could not have foreseen the trap they were laying for the future as the reach of PDDs was unknown.

Crystal-Dawn had a much deeper connection with Gerrasimos than even he knew. He did things that literally made him the perfect man for her. It wasn't just that he could use a chainsaw either. Previously, Crystal had viewed the use of a chainsaw to be the manliest of activities since it was the only "manly" activity she had been fearful to try. It was a giant spinning, toothed weapon—without a guard that could remove human limbs with greater ease than the resistance offered from a tree. Chainsaws are to be greatly respected, and anyone capable of safely using such a terrifying tool deserves huge respect. Gerrasimos used a sixty-inch bar on his chainsaw when Crystal met him. She felt he was her light.

So it was when the sea had finally settled,
The waves rested, the turmoil dissipated,
That an incredible light broke through.
Creating a glow and warmth never before felt.
A sky once thought clear was now illuminated, clearing the stagnant, suffocating haze.
Possibilities abound, those thought too big, or impossible, now all become choices.

Light has a way of changing that which it touches.
How a landscape can flourish with light!
It creates growth, sustains life, eliminates darkness.
The light does not tell the landscape to change,
It merely provides the opportunity by giving of itself.
The two-edged sword is splitting, for light cannot always shine and in the absence of light, the darkness is deafening.

A feverish faith the light will return,
Time is hurried by preparing for its arrival.
A time of warmth, comfort, and clarity.
For once the landscape blooms it becomes dependent on the light,
And though it can withstand the darkness of night,
It is by the grace of dawn that beautiful growth can occur once more.

May 10, 2022

Today Gerrasimos and Crystal were traveling to the family farm. They needed to empty some possessions out of the home, or they would be tossed. There wouldn't be much time for writing during the day. It ended up being a lot more than expected. It ended up being the fateful day that they were to take any valuables of Grandma because the old farmhouse was getting cleaned up for occupancy. Grandma never returned to sort through her possessions after being taken to a home. It had been years and the mice and rats had their way with everything. The risk of the hantavirus was present, but they were not there to clean and stir the dust, merely find the hidden gems of a sixty-year-old time capsule. Gerrasimos's intention was to help his mom in any way needed and clear his own few furniture items out. His mom's intention was to clean out any of her mother's personal records. Crystal's intention was to ensure the history was preserved.

She started with the old photos. Those were obvious to see the importance. The first item to catch her eye was a book. That's right, Crystal found God. There it was, an old yet well-cared-for copy of

The Truth That Leads to Eternal Life. It was an old Jehovah's Witness hardcover book copyrighted in 1968. These books were no longer in publication. Of course, Crystal used to have an extensive library of such books, typically highlighted with notes. This was not the copy of someone who had studied it thoroughly of course. It was a seed that had been planted, just waiting for someone to find it. Then there were several old leather-bound books. These thrilled Crystal to no end. There were so many Bibles. A typewriter was acquired along with a couple of ottomans to match Grandma's chair Crystal was now using as her writing chair. She didn't actually sit in chairs. She perched like a bird. Curled up with her knees outward, offering a shield and armrest. It seemed odd other people didn't sit this way, made it a lot easier to move about in a moment. She likened sitting to a Bible story where a soldier sat by a riverbank. Some of the men stuck their heads in the water to drink and were unaware of what occurred around them. The smart soldier collected the water in his hand and brought it to his mouth to drink, so he could be aware of his surroundings, in constant awareness. That constant awareness was being lost in people. So lost in their own thoughts, seldom are people aware of their surroundings. After a long day of moving furniture about, packing boxes, and filling garbage bags, a few more gems had been found that would really make the day hugely significant. A dresser containing the key to save the farm was found. It was not a literal key but contained so many files and documents. This dresser in its entirety would provide what was needed for the farm to be registered as a heritage site and qualify for all the funding available to the special places and people that helped build a community.

Why was this farm so significant to the Village of Lumby? Frank had moved up from Langley in the sixties and bought a farm. His brother bought one too, and they traded work back and forth getting everyone established. Frank also had a logging company and had many men working for him. He dreamed of creating a home in the country for people that couldn't afford to buy their own farms. He built the Trinity Mobile Home Park. An old advertisement found had a picture of a young girl with pigtails, curled up in the long grass petting a baby sheep. It read, "We specialize in Country Living." There was an old colored photo attached at the bottom showing the farm and trailer park as an aerial view. There appeared to be approximately sixty-five trailer homes in view. There are now at least eighty homes in 2022. One of the residents is even a family member! These individuals are the people of Lumby. Some have saved enough to purchase their own trailer; some are just renting, seeking an affordable home. Small towns in BC were somewhat protected from some of the proles as not many proles had their own transportation and therefore needed to live closer to the welfare offices, true story. They didn't have the means to live in the country if they couldn't get into town to fill out paperwork when required and pick up checks. As anyone on the system knew, though not required monthly to be at the office in person, something came up typically that would require standing in line for the dole. This trailer park was and is an opportunity for lower-income families to live in an outdoor, farm-like setting, nestled into the foot of the once forested, now clear-cut, pillaged mountainside.

These individuals would benefit greatly from having the Village of Lumby purchase the farm and use it to preserve the history of the family and offer gardening space to residents and a creek to play in come summertime. This was Crystal's dream for the farm.

There was a book, which came to Crystal as nothing more than mere chance. This book was the Book of Life. This book gave her all the power she ever needed for all her time and would need to be entrusted to someone upon her passing. If there ever was such thing as a witch, this made Crystal one without any proper training or knowledge. She held all the tools required now to do what needed to be done. The day before, the indigenous manifesto had come to her along with a clay drum, stretched with rawhide. The day before that she had learned how to bend a spoon with her mind, simply by explaining it to her daughter. When one explains something in simple terms to another, they sometimes reach realizations never before known while already having carried the information in pieces without ever having seen the big picture.

Would you like to know how to bend a spoon with your mind? It turned out Crystal's children had never seen the *Matrix* and had no idea what she meant about a spoon because she had been holding a phone charging cord the whole time she spoke. It started when the youngest approached Crystal while she was charging in the sun. If you catch a crystal while it was fully charged, you get the best radiation! Well, her daughter was upset because her phone charger had been pulled apart and would not work. She was devastated, holding the exposed wires with small soldered connection points. Although reassured there were other cords, this had been her first cord for her first cell phone. She assigned a lot of personal value to her possessions, which was nice to see the appreciation of financial value. There was a point where objects should not hold such sway over a person's emotions. Crystal then explained how to bend a spoon with one's mind, "This cord, held out in hand, was not a saddening broken cord. It was an exciting piece of scientific discovery that could now be taken apart to see how it operates!" Her daughter's mood lightened at the thought of getting to pull it apart as she still enjoyed being a scientist in her free time. Usually, she was doing chemistry experiments as a slime movement swept through the young people. It was in explaining this though that Crystal-Dawn herself realized the power of her words. She too had an experience that day, the feeling of being filled with hope, just to discover it was a misread name. She had spent the great majority of that day in a state of hopefulness before realizing her personal blunder. Why did she need someone else to fill her with hope? She didn't. She had enough hope herself that she could quite easily bend that spoon to her will. There were enough negative naysayers in the world and that path was not an option. It was the hopeless option of doom.

These books offered insight though that Crystal-Dawn needed to tie everything together to make logical sense to the people. Gerrasimos was always telling her she needed to be more clear. Last night their study of the chakras made Crystal realize she had no interest whatsoever anymore in that color palate of the individual. She knew those colors. It was a lovely rainbow, and she felt it through and through. The unknown to be explored was what was beyond the rainbow. There's a lot more to rainbows than you may be aware of. When light is refracted, it makes more than one rainbow. There are other rainbows all around seldom seen as more than a flicker of light in the blinding sun. Gerrasimos had once joined Crystal in the sun. She silenced him and asked him to join her in her headspace. He closed his eyes and they rested their heads together. The sun was not as brilliant as it had once been. Clouds rolled across the sky as evening approached and the sun bid adieu. She played a song and they sat listening, eyes closed.

>Sunshine on my shoulders makes me happy
>Sunshine in my eyes can make me cry
>Sunshine on the water looks so lovely
>Sunshine almost always makes me high
>If I had a day that I could give you
>I'd give to you a day just like today
>If I had a song that I could sing for you, I'd sing a song
>to make you feel this way.
>Sunshine on my shoulders.
>(John Denver)

Crystal-Dawn loved Gerrasimos to the fullest extent of her being. She knew she had found her twin flame. He didn't believe in it though. It was not her, but there is the idea that there are souls in this world that complete each other and were meant to find each other throughout time. The most fortunate enough to have ever gained the loving favor of another are aware you can love many throughout your lifetime. These past loves do not lessen the love of the present. Relationships help people grow. People need people to grow. This is a fact. A child raised without contact with other people was how mankind was before they evolved with communication. A hermit living in the woods has similar experiences day in and day out. These are experiences of survival, getting food, cooking food, eating food, getting firewood, and maintaining a fire for the food and heat. There is also the keeping of a shelter for safety and storage. After that there is merely fending off predators and maintaining hygiene. Was this truly the desired height of humanity now in 2022? This is to get away from the world (i.e., each other) and live a life of solitude because your relationship won't last, parents are too demanding, and children won't listen or even talk anymore? Gerrasimos had a dream to head in that direction. Out on land where he could build whatever he wanted and collect building materials without anyone's complaint of useless hoarding. Crystal too wanted to be on land, so they were a perfect fit, both willing to do the work of the pioneers to create a homestead and sustain themselves with their own efforts. Have you ever thought you really wanted something, desired it, worked for it, attained it just to realize you don't really want it? This was Crystal's greatest fear for how she spent her time. After all, time is the currency of your life. What if you spent it poorly? The present consciousness only has eighty to one hundred years of time if we're lucky to experience all that life has to offer. Each experience helps an individual to grow to a higher state of enlightenment and connectedness. Crystal feared if she got her dream of living in the woods, she would not find peace because the rest of the world would still be in pain. How could one possibly skip through the forest with a free light heart, at one with the universe, knowing full well how much pain the universe was in? Ignoring the pain of those around you crying out for help are not the means to have an enlightened soul. If your physical partner by your side carried the pains of the whole world, you would do whatever was in your power to help them. The whole world was crying out, and Sri Krishna promised his return when the world needed him. A human's lifespan is only so long, and each day is a gift.

What if these long days blended into months that sped by into forgotten years that felt like an overall waste in the end upon review? There were countless stories of irritable people, angry with the world for how their life went. A most inspirational song was written that helped people see past their own misery and stand up for themselves.

> Yeah, I get it, you're an outcast, always under attack, always coming in last, bringing up the past.
>
> No one owes you anything, I think you need a shotgun blast, a kick in the ass, so paranoid, watch your back!
>
> Oh my, here we go, another loose cannon gone bipolar, slipped down, couldn't get much lower.
>
> Quicksand's got no sense of humor, I'm still laughing like hell
>
> You think that by cryin' to me, lookin' so sorry, that I'm gonna believe you've been infected by a social disease; well, then, take your medicine.
>
> I created the Sound of Madness, wrote the book on pain, somehow I'm still here, to explain;
>
> That the darkest hour never comes in the night, you can sleep with a gun, but when you gonna wake up and fight . . . For yourself?
>
> (Shinedown, "Sound of Madness")

That was the problem with society in 2022. Despite being a partially free, yet divided world, people weren't actually allowed to speak up for themselves anymore. The Truckers Protest in Canada was a perfect example. The extreme violence used against anti-mandate peaceful demonstrators in New Zealand was an even more extreme example. Better yet, the world gathered in Beijing, China, and public politicians warned athletes not to speak up and get involved in Chinese affairs.

"Abuses committed included mass arbitrary detention, torture, enforced disappearances, mass surveillance, cultural and religious persecution, separation of families, forced returns to China, forced labor, and sexual violence and violations of reproductive rights. Little news trickled out of Xinjiang in 2021, however, as the authorities maintained tight control over information, and as access to the region, already limited, was further constrained due to Covid-19 movement restrictions.

"New research from AidData revealed US$385 billion in 'hidden debt' owed by developing countries to Chinese authorities.

"Authorities banned the annual Victoria Park vigil commemorating victims of the 1989 Tiananmen Square massacre in Beijing. On the day of the vigil, police arrested the vice-chair of the organizing group, Hong Kong Alliance, cordoned off the park, and stationed officers throughout the city to prevent remembrances. In September, police froze the Alliance's HK$2.2 million (US$283,000) in assets, closed its June 4th Museum about the massacre, revoked its registration, deleted its social media accounts, and arrested its four leaders for 'inciting subversion.'

"Police censored the internet through website blocking for the first time" (Human Rights Watch, "2022 World Report").

May 11, 2022

Crystal-Dawn had a whirlwind of spiritual development with the arrival of these new books in her life. One particular favorite was the Holy Bible. It read, "Containing the Old and New Testaments Translated out of the Original Tongues and with the former Translations diligently compared and revised by His Majesty's special command, AD 1611—Appointed to be read in Churches." Crystal had grown up studying the New World Translation and had never had the opportunity to read the closest thing mankind had to the original Bible in English. THIS was EPIC! She flipped around to the various memorized scriptures in her head. For the last eighteen years, she had thought this knowledge useless and tried to push it from her mind. Matthew 24:14, Psalm 83:18, Romans 10:13, or was it 1 Corinthians? Her mind was spewing forth words and numbers with the fluidity of a forgotten language. She lingered a little with James, visited the Corinthians, then dove into Revelation. It was amazing how understandable Old English was easily translated to be understood. Was it perhaps her recent readings of George Orwell, Jonathan Swift, and other old texts that had primed her mind to read this Bible with such great understanding? It was as if all her prior knowledge of God had been collectively added to a large equation of knowledge that was being sorted to make sense in such a way that it all tied together and supported one another.

It served a purpose. Gerrasimos was not raised with any spirituality in his life. In his experience, the church was something that some of the business owners attended to socialize with other business owners in town. To not be part of the churches would be more difficult to build a thriving business. After all, it was the people in the congregations that created the towns that were the necessary clients to conduct business. Crystal-Dawn had been raised in a very tight-knit, religious community that taught God came before employment as employment was a means to earn a living so one could pursue their true purpose of serving God. That meant worshipping Him. Broken down further to plain English—He is our Father and wants exactly what any Father wants. He wants respect. He wants to be recognized for His efforts. He wants His creations to be enjoyed and appreciated by all (the Earth, the animals, the plants, etc.). He wants His children to get along, most definitely not to kill each other. Squabbling is almost expected in a family though still offers annoyance to a father who does so much work.

In the Old Testament, God is not the same one depicted in the New Testament. He softened. Like an aging man, He softened. The youth of man have been known for their vigor and willingness to hunt or test each other physically through wrestling. They even take up arms for justice and be willing to slay an unknown enemy of the people they have not personally known. As age and experience weigh down a man's soul, it softens as did God's throughout the story of the Bible. He went from wanting to take an eye for an eye to suggesting you turn the other cheek when you have received injury. He even sent his son to tell all the people of the Earth this precious hope that would one day help free them of the chains of the old system of things.

Crystal-Dawn needed to finish writing *Animal Farm Part II* so people everywhere could see what was right in front of them. There were literally rainbows everywhere the light touched. It was from the energy of the sun radiated through the hydrating moisture that filled the air that also filled the lungs of the people, for of course everything was connected. Rainbows were everywhere and sometimes you just needed someone to point them out. The question remained; would the people be willing to come outside in the rain to see the rainbow? Its true brilliance was dulled through the panes of glass the people looked through from indoors. Everyone claimed to have seen the rainbow or at least had seen one in the past so they did not need to rise from their comfortable chairs to see THIS rainbow.

It was a personal belief held by Crystal that the people didn't want to get wet or were fearful the rain may be too poisoned from the industrial efforts of a few. Perhaps they did not want to be grounded to the earth. Crystal could relate. She didn't want to be grounded either until she was ready and fought it frequently throughout the day by bouncing about. She felt if she stood still, her energy would drain out of her feet. The doctors said it was orthopedic hypotension or blood pooling and not circulating to the legs. Standing still led to a path of lightheadedness, then dizziness, then fainting. Since she typically also didn't eat throughout the day, there were enough medical causes to contradict Crystal's belief in grounding. Whether her bouncing sway kept her blood circulating or eliminated the grounding effects of standing still, she understood the desire to keep her energy flowing within and not release it to the earth.

Surely this machine needed to be fixed because mankind could not stay indoors for the rest of their existence. Neither could they yet flee to another planet. The Earth was their mother, and they could not leave her. They were connected.

Chapter 4

The Meeting of the Nations

The crystal was only one crystal, and there were many other frequencies that needed to be heard to resonate throughout the nations. The knowledge of the chakras was bestowed upon the doves. Nobody thought such simple birds of no color would carry the knowledge of all the colored energy frequencies of the universe. That was what white was though, didn't you know? It was all the colors of light. Other birds had heard of the knowledge of the chakras and bore the colors of the birds of paradise. They were lovely in their passion for the truth, but some failed to grasp the deeper meaning behind it. They could bend their bodies in unique ways though to open chakras through physical movement. The animals needed physical items to connect their thoughts because the power of thought had been taken over by man. The thoughts of men—fear, anger, lust, greed, gluttony, pride, and selfishness—filled the animals' minds. The few centimeters inside their skull were no longer their own as they had chosen to let the PDDs fill their minds because they didn't want to think. It hurt. Neither did they want to physically move about and exercise as that hurt too. The majority of animals sought a life of comfort and ease. They failed to understand their bodies were created as that of their mother that had requirements to live. Their hearts were pumps that worked by constricting the muscles throughout their body. Without the movement of all the muscles, the blood could not pump effectively. The animals were not only dying, but living pain-induced lives from the poisons that filled them and the lack of physical activity, being chained to a PDD. It was believed the animals could handle at least seven and a half hours of being chained to a PDD with no physical requirement than the occasional muscle constrictions of one's fingers to type. If the animals refused to be chained to the PDDs, they were refused food, water, and shelter—the basic physical requirements of life. With this base chakra being in a constant state of turmoil, the animals could not balance themselves or their lives. They could not seek enlightenment or connect with others as these skills were not acquired until one had first balanced their heart chakra.

The crystal needed all the crystals to vibrate at all frequencies to unite all the animals. The meeting was merely a meeting of the nations. Appointed by some animals, exactly how unknown as the animals never held a general meeting to vote anymore, the leaders of the United Nations were merely animals too. Some were there trying to create a better world for all animals. Some were there by duty to appear as though they were striving for a better world too. These were the leaders that typically did not even show up for the important meetings of change. Even when they did meet, the only thing agreed upon was that a change needed to be made, and sometime in the future, it would occur. A young badger once approached them and scolded their lack of effort. This was their responsibility for the position they carried, yet they would not act. Just as the historic *Titanic* had once represented the world, and offered insights to be learned from, the majority of leaders were more interested in the treasures that lay within than the stories of those who perished. The crystal was first asked to swear that its statements would be truthful. It refused to swear upon one book alone but made an oath to the people,

> I cross my heart, and promise to give all I've got to give
> to make all your dreams come true.
>
> In all the world, you'll never find a love as true as mine.

You will always be the miracle, that makes my life complete, and as long as there's a breath in me, I'll make yours just as sweet.

As we look into the future, It's as far as we can see.

So let's make each tomorrow be the best that it can be.

I cross my heart, and promise to give all I've got to give to make all your dreams come true.

In all the world, you'll never find, a love as true as mine.

(George Strait, "I Cross My Heart")

Other singers stepped forth before the United Nations and their voices rang out around the globe to all animals.

The Innocents

It was the innocents locked in the hull that perished that should have been remembered. Locked behind the iron gates of the *Titanic*, they perished because the upper class was comfortable. The upper class could have easily saved themselves and yet even they didn't have the common sense to forgo comfort for survival. The lower classes below had little choice. The truth of the ship's sinking had been hidden until the icy waters of the Atlantic were pouring into their rooms and drowning their children. I'm sure when it first began, they were probably told it was just a burst pipe and just calm down and relax because maintenance would arrive (which were the trade animals themselves) once it had been reviewed and approved by the upper class. As we know with all bureaucracies, if it doesn't suit their needs at that time, it was not approved. The innocents died while the ruling comfortable few continued their lives of leisure.

The animals recognized this life of leisure. The middle class of animals, the ones right below the main level of the machine, had received the scraps of food and knew of its true goodness. They could see the light and feel its power from time to time. There were just small beams of light that filtered through the rickety machine. The scaffolding around the heart had aged and occasionally pieces would break off, killing a few innocent animals below. The main offices of the governments and organizations were on the top floor. Access was restricted of course. The lower levels slowly deteriorated to the extent that if you entered the ground floor, you would be stupefied. Animals were not allowed to enter these lower levels either. Access was denied except to the specialized crew that did the annual shutdown cleanup/maintenance check.

It was in these times that the vermin or animals that had slipped through the cracks were exterminated. Whether it was public knowledge or not was unknown as the majority of animals didn't want to think about it. It was sad and they felt there was nothing they could do anyway. Those who did care about the state of disrepair of the machine were told they could only care about a few specialized problems and were then directed to the organization that had been put in place to deal with that issue. The animals did not want their comfort tainted with negativity as they knew the effect it had on their chakras, so they called the problems issues and were, therefore, less negative and more tolerable to discuss over tea. Tensions in the Middle East had created the need for more energy. Then in the war, the Soviets killed animals in the name of animals. Hell, they had an entire floor dedicated to controlling the animals' workforce to use up resources with objects of war and then blow them up or sink them in the oceans, adding even more poison to the water. The machine that was created to control the Earth's heart and drain her body of her resources was created with the thoughts of men and fueled by the animals' own energy.

How would they ever deal with such an intricate machine that all life balanced on? So many futures could be seen that surely led to the collapse of the lungs or perhaps liver failure. The machine had taken the fruitage of the spirit, fermented it, and fed it back to the animals.

Crystal-Dawn stopped to rest and think. Her head still ached daily, the pain gradually increasing throughout the day to becoming a roar of mixed frequencies in her head. So many clear different sounds could be heard; she could almost individually mimic their sounds like a bird with different calls. She had always had one frequency which she had been explaining was the sound of her heart pushing blood past her ears. That was normal. It was not an ear pain like that of an earache and hearing was unaffected. One was an unusually sharp, constant sound. It was the most unbearable.

She gathered her crystals and set her intentions. She called upon and used the power of Africa. Africa was mighty and seeped in the blood of the innocents. Her totem was an ebony statue her adopted father had given her. She had added the chakra color points for visual connection purposes. The statue was an African individual holding a rock tall above their head. Crystal-Dawn had little interest in the rainbow chakra typical of those interested in self-balance. Crystal cared more for the chakras of the third eye and up into the universe of connectedness. Her interest did not stem as far as the depths of the universe and all it had to offer. Her intent was to connect with the people around her, her partner, her children, her family, her neighbors, and the whole world. Someone was required to step into the limelight and say, "It can be done." Considering a man like Jesus could come into this world with such a message of love, of forgiveness, and not be accepted but rather be crucified was clear evidence no one could ever rise that could unite all people, wasn't it? Those were the thoughts of men, self-doubt, fear for surely mankind had the power to create whatever world they wanted. Whatever they thought, they could speak in words that started the process of bringing thoughts into reality.

This idea of bringing thoughts into reality was their little piece of God. He had made people in His image and within each person is God. It was not that they are God, but rather having some of His power, that being life. Life gave us the ability to grow so we could learn and have experiences which in turn help us grow until hopefully by the end of a long joyful experience we can retire in peace and enjoy the long-earned sleep of a satisfied and complete soul. It was one that experienced all life had to offer and lived as many lives as possible within the time their consciousness allowed. Crystal looked at the lines on her Lemurian seed crystal. She had known absolutely nothing about crystals or believed in their power until three days ago when Gerrasimos and her watched a blue cartoon man explain scientifically how crystals work with geometric shapes. She saw one image and was an immediate believer. It was so similar to the pattern of light she saw that connected all living things on the earth. It could have been it. It was hard to say though as there had been so many lines connecting so many things. Early spring was so rich with life. Perhaps fall and winter would offer a different view. She had temporarily borrowed her daughters' crystals to see what she thought of them. The video said, "Try one and see if you notice a difference in that area." Well, back when Crystal had gone to Africa, she carried her daughter's crystal with her. She had accidentally broken part of it so had kept it in safe keeping. It came to her that upon gathering these crystals, she carried these blue and clear crystals for some time and had an amazing ability to communicate quite clearly. Whether it was the crystals or the dialectic behavior therapy techniques for communicating with others, she had the strength of communication.

When she shopped for her own crystals, at first, she cared not for the names and descriptions of the gems, but rather to which she was attracted. She then realized if she wanted the crystals to work for her, she would need to be a proper friend and get to know them. The crystals were officially future friends she hadn't met yet. She began choosing her friends wisely. These were the friends that would help guide her character and spirit in her intentions.

The first was a bloodstone—centering.

"Bloodstone is excellent for centering and grounding. It is said to help with calming, particularly in survival situations. It is said to be a stone of courage, bringing mental, physical and emotional renewal by releasing blockages. It is said to be particularly good for helping emotional traumas and grief."

The second was a carnelian—courage.

"Carnelian is an agate class of chalcedony that is a stone of Creativity, Individuality and Courage. Like all agates, it has protection energies.

Carnelian can help ease or remove sorrows. It also helps stabilize energies in the home. It is also a stone of protection in general and from anger, jealousy and fear. In addition it can help with manifestation of one's desires, and brings good luck."

The third was a honey calcite—amplifier.

As if she needed amplifying, Gerrasimos picked one also with rainbows deep beneath its surface.

"Honey Calcite is a stone that gently amplifies energy. It also assists in the challenges associated with change. Honey Calcite enhances psychic abilities, astral projection and higher consciousness. It also enhances intellect and memory."

Could there have been a more perfect stone for the two of them as partners and also individually?

The fourth was two stones as Crystal loved green the most and wanted to especially enhance her heart]s loving power.

Rain forest jasper—nature

"The earth stone makes a wonderful connection to earth and all its inhabitants—plant, mineral, and animal. It brings awareness and joy for the natural state of things, such as your own body, and emotional balance. It is an excellent stone for communication with animals or totems."

Kambaba jasper—peace

"Kambaba Jasper is a stone of peace, tranquility, and fertility. It reminds us of the gift of life and our connection to all living things of the present, past & future. Rich in orbs and swirls of green and black, this stone is commonly used to aid in mediation."

The fifth was a blue apatite—personal power.

"Blue Apatite is a dual-action stone, known for its positive use of personal power to achieve goals. It clears away confusion, apathy or negativity, then. Stimulates the intellect to expand knowledge and truth, which may be used for personal growth or for the collective good.

It is a Stone of Manifestation, promoting a humanitarian outlook and service to others."

She did not purchase the sixth but continued to use her daughter's stone as a temporary loan, but she loved having her involvement.

The seventh was special. It was a super seven—a higher purpose.

"The Super Seven Crystal represents the universal brotherhood of humanity. Super Seven Crystals provide an access corridor to the subconscious mind to re-remember why you are here, what your role is, and how you can live that purpose to its highest degree. Super Seven retains all the properties of Amethyst, Clear Quartz, Smoky Quartz, Cacoxenite, Rutile, Geothite, and Lepidocrocite combined. This is one of the few stones that retains all the energy and clarity of each mineral and it never needs cleansing or energizing!"

Crystal-Dawn gathered her intentions. The sun shone its light with great strength at her back, casting rainbows everywhere. It was near impossible to see the computer screen, but Crystal needed to continue the story so the people would understand the smallest of changes that were needed to create the change that saved the world. Everyone knew we were living in the times of the end and had been waiting with a tombstone mentality that there was an afterlife. and it would set them free. Or that if they prayed enough, God would come as promised and fix everything. They just didn't know when. It made sense though. If the homeowner knew the hour of the thief's arrival, he would have been alert to it. When Crystal was thrown off a cliff as a child twice, her brother prayed for her. He failed to recognize the power to save his sister. It was in fact in his own hands. Had he prayed out loud for all to hear, they could have answered his prayers and leaped to save her. It was the god within each of us that people were not speaking to and therefore could not answer each other's prayers.

The Bible crystal had acquired was wonderful. As with all the old books she was now the caretaker of, she held them gently, feeling their covers, imagining their past lives and adventures. *Who had held this book?* Surely all that had held it had at one time had these same words echo through their consciousness. This Bible in particular was the book of a preacher. It was not a fact but believed to be true. Among the old books was a diary of Mary Beach from 1923. Beautifully handwritten words lined the pages with delicate notes of her life. How many eggs the chicken lay, sales of eggs, visiting of neighbors, the weather, her health, and fasting, but most importantly, who she referred to as father but was believed to be her husband Enos who regularly left and returned and was regularly at church more than weekly, sometimes every third day. At one point in her diary, she was healed and no longer required reading glasses. She died the following year and this diary was the only connection to know about her as 1924 was a long time ago in anyone's memory.

Gerrasimos entered the room with delight in his eyes to find Crystal-Dawn sprawled out on animal furs, topless, bathing in sunlight and rainbows literally. Despite having all her words gathered to write, being on a roll with thought and words that most certainly needed to be written, she cheerily leaped to his side for she so loved him. Despite living together and working together, they didn't spend every moment together. He had his own dealings in the backyard/compound/zoo/building site of their future home/time and business investment/funding for the future to care for. There was so much more value in a square foot of land than most people knew.

After what felt like an hour, Crystal-Dawn had come to a lot of realizations that needed to be recorded. These days every moment that occurred was another wonderful realization of understanding that led to peace, joy, and love that continued to create yet another ripple. Each of these ripples like the shapes within the super-seven gem was repeating. Everything fell into these same patterns repeating throughout the universe, throughout time.

An example of this would be the smaller world within a world that c—

Ahh, her mind had difficulty collecting all the thoughts with the occurrences and the actual physical writing of the words in such a way to be understood.

You see after her partner had come, she was trying to explain both the experiences with him and after he left. Then her daughter came to visit but with the most intense negative of energies. She had calmed her and then understood the situation, gave wise advice for action with positive intent, and then her friend she was distressing about called! You see she had worried herself to a point of serious concern, and she could hear it in her voice. Her friend was elated to have gotten her phone back and wanted to plan to go swimming and hang out. Her daughter still displayed odd energy, so Crystal radiated some joy and positivity, and her daughter was set to have a great time.

She was all set to write about the experiences when her daughter returned to discuss nuances of her planned adventure when Crystal set her bounds that she had done her duty healing and talking and if this was trivial and unrelated to her that she would not be giving of her time or head space.

That was one of the realizations. Focus.

Headspace is the few centimeters of space in your head that belongs to you. George Orwell described the space of consciousness quite well. That was one of the beautiful things about the past. They simplified everything to reduce the speaking of unnecessary words. There used to be a purpose in communication. One spoke to another to convey a thought, ask a question, inform, describe, etc. There was an intention. Even if the speaking of words was small talk between individuals, it would be for the purpose of spreading pleasantries. That does not mean that bad did not exist for surely one of the communications would be to sound warning would it not? That was so primal it was already in the sound base of the human brain. Humans of any language could speak to one another through a variety of means that spoke to the soul and not the brain.

Cats and dogs, the lessons they offer in subjection by will versus force, one is more pleasing than the other, but both are valued by people. Some people wanted to earn the love of their pet, some wanted easy love that could be instilled with force or treats.

Crystal-Dawn realized what was occurring and how to fix it. You see it is quite difficult to exist in different planes of existence let alone be able to stop and write about the balance occurring at all times between thinking (a mental state) and doing (a physical state). Not many could balance this task simultaneously and required a complete concentration to do one or the other. Now add emotion to any of this, and it adds a color of energy to which to view the situation, a different perspective from the same spot just through a different lens of color. Crystal had that ability, the ability to not only multitask the thinking and doing but also simultaneously change her lens of perspective based on the color of emotion. This color range of the chakra, once known to Crystal, finally made sense and connected the energy that could be felt by another person. Not all colors are visibly seen, but their energies can be felt by others. The secret to "seeing" someone's aurora is as simple as discerning what state of perspective the other person was in. If they were caught on their physical primal needs, they typically glowed red. Sexually aroused people are not necessarily orange but a blend of various colors depending on the connectedness between individuals. Loving people who spoke to you with open hearts glowed a natural green, but sometimes pink as there was an outer chakra in front of a person. Wise-minded were blue and open-minded were purple. Simple connections once made were seen everywhere because the human brain does that. It believes; it creates.

She didn't have time to ponder on the feelings and colors of when she conjured a storm, but truly this was one day worth considering so she could perhaps not draw off its energies intentionally but know of them so as to avoid them.

Many assumed that the one who could unite mankind must be spotless, without sin, be washed white in the blood of the lamb, but have we not already established that white is in fact all the colors? Had mankind grown so keen on the idea that white meant clean and spotless rather than the full spectrum of colors we now know it to be?

We know no man was without the stain of sin. The purpose of experience was to help individuals grow to enlightenment throughout their existence. Just as boiling water can soften a potato or harden an egg, so too bad experiences could influence how the individual responds to the pressure. Remember crystals are formed under great amounts of heat energy and pressure. They form as they do because they are the material they are made of, the external pressures placed upon them to become a strengthened, crystalized version of themselves in pure geometric, universe-aligned shapes. We all grow under pressure. Another parable would be a sword and a stone. A stone can beat a sword and damage the blade, or the blade can hit the stone in such motions as to sharpen the blade. Gerrasimos commonly called Crystal-Dawn a double-edged blade as she could seriously draw blood. She had been finely tuned and sharpened over time by each experience she encountered. She was ready and she knew she could handle what was to come as long as her family was safe.

It was already 9:30 p.m. and the sun had set. The coolness of the evening was felt in the air, and it was evident the day was drawing to an end. Tomorrow she would tell of the power of Africa that was bestowed upon her. Tonight, her mind would sort the past, present, and future to best explain to the people how they could create the change. Tomorrow was the day she would tell how the animals fixed the world. Today her time had ended, and the resonating shape of the super seven crystal lay embedded in her mind. At the center was herself, and the five-sided shape continued in larger and larger repeating patterns like a Russian doll with a tiny baby at the center. It was a perfect replica of the largest and each repeating size smaller. This was our universe. If she could fix a small-scale version of a problem, the same solution could be magnified for the equating larger version of the problem. It was simple and made perfect sense. The lessons of the past had to be used to plan the future so the present would know what actions needed to be taken.

George Orwell said, "He who controls the past, controls the future, he who controls the present controls the past."

Crystal-dawn had old books in her possession that gave her power of the past in text.

She carried the power of the people of the past in their stories, long scribed in her memory and could be recalled as if from a conversation with a friend from a moment ago.

She carried the power of Africa and the innocents lost in corruption. Not only did she carry the spirits of the dead innocents, but she also carried the physical burden of proof of existence and experience. She had not known the significance at the time but upon later review discovered the depth of what had occurred. If we simply stated, Crystal was awarded the opportunity to travel to Africa, that in itself would be of amazement due to her social status and finances. When the details unfold of how a humanitarian was able to be awarded permission to enter a country that was experiencing turmoil, mass murder, and mass corruption at the start of a global health pandemic was not only awe-inspiring but also horrifying. That was for tomorrow though.

Balance in doing all the things was required for this intention.

May 12, 2022
Africa

    Cameroon, Africa. This is a special soul story that is not recommended to be repeated by others. These stories typically end in a woman being sold into the sex trade. In 2017, Crystal-Dawn met a friend online. They were both members of a Facebook taxidermy group. She thought his name was Tonye for years, literally years, being unaware in Africa they write their last name first and the first name last. In the beginning, Crystal loved the idea of having a friend in Africa. He was born exactly six months after her. He sent photos at first, but they were always of poor quality. The name he used at that time on the first account was Vamoulké. It didn't mean anything to Crystal-Dawn until years later when she found out who Vamoulké was, and it was quite fitting that Paul had been working for Vamoulké's release. Amadou Vamoulké was a Cameroonian journalist that was being held in prison for years. Even the UN had asked for his release. He was a good man that was fighting for the people's rights.

    At that time Crystal was in a relationship with a movie star/world champion and was in the process of taking apart her business to relocate to Alberta. Paul was a perfect gentleman that never crossed the flirtation line and treated Crystal as an actual person. They remained friends, talking occasionally for years. Crystal had moved to Alberta in March and returned to British Columbia in May. By late summer, their friendship had grown into an online romance. Online relationships are quite common these days. They offer the opportunity to meet people more similar to yourself without the restrictions of local availability. The more diverse people are, the more difficult it is to find similarities. Although when matched with an opposite with similar goals, these two individuals have the power to support one another to no end.

    This perfect matching of opposites is challenging as the two are each other's strengths where they are weak, but also the proof of why they need to try to positively influence their partner. Men and women had biological differences that gave each their own superpowers.

These are heightened abilities of nature. Typically being women could be more empathetic, healing, and offer an emotional way of thinking while men could offer physical security and a more logic-based way of thinking. When these two influence each other, they offer insight into a heightened, more diverse being or character. Both men and women carried the ability to be both emotional and physical in all their activities but needed each other to grow. This is where human connectedness is important. Without it we are merely surviving alone in nature, interacting with God's creations. Even God Himself sought companionship in heaven. Crystal-Dawn pondered what made a person a good person. There were a variety of responses from people. Crystal believed it was in how we treat each other as people. It was helping others, being kind, saying positive encouraging things, or even just being a listening ear and showing interest in the person and their story. But what would happen if you relocated that person to the middle of the forest. There are no other people around. Then what would make them a good person? She imagined that person who lived in harmony with nature would be a good person. The bad person would be perceived as the one that was destroying the forest, so the other animals lost their homes and food. If she could be a good person in the forest, then she would create a small space for herself, no bigger than necessary, and spend her days caring for the animals and plants. She would try to create small homes in the dead branches with fluffy grasses. Perhaps she would remove the bark from a decayed tree so the birds could access the bugs beneath its tough exterior. There wasn't too much that could be done to help that did not hinder the life of another living species. Just walking upon the forest floor, she was killing the moss and fungi itself trying to grow upon it.

One did not realize the life under their feet until one lies on the ground and stares at its beauty in wonder. Moss was an entire miniature ecosystem that looked like an alien planet you would see in a movie. Sometimes Crystal would find an ant struggling alone to move a giant seed. She would search the ground for another ant to join in the efforts of moving the seed. It didn't always work trying to get random ants to work together, but sometimes it did. Those were the moments that made it worthwhile finding the ant a friend to help carry the load.

Greatest of apologies, let's go back to Africa. It was in the fall of 2019 that Crystal-Dawn booked a trip to Cameroon. She may have found the cost overwhelming had she researched all the costs upfront, but she did not. She had a habit of leaping based on faith and not fact. The flight was affordable and made possible by a baby bear taxidermy mount for a trapper that had found it in the snow walking his line. It was an epic piece that paid for the flight. Then the cost of a visa, for Cameroon was a country that required special permission to travel to, Paul had to get a letter of permission from their police for Crystal to be able to enter the country.

She really wanted to tour the fur tanneries in Douala, but to prearrange such meetings meant she was trying to conduct business and must be mentioned. To avoid such headaches, she never got to see the tanneries but would do so one day in an effort to help them reduce pollution caused by tanning agents used in the chemical processes of tanning leather. Ah yes, that's right, Crystal-Dawn is a humanitarian/environmentalist/animal rights activist that at that time had been working as the first female flesher in the Okanagan Valley of British Columbia, Canada. That's a title she holds proudly as fleshing is the most advanced skill required in a tannery. This skill dates back to the beginning of time as men used animal skins for a body covering for as long as we were aware. She was self-taught with most skills until others helped impart their wisdom along the way. Had it not been for a retired fire chief/trapper in Prince George, she would not have understood what the old books were explaining about how to turn ears, noses, and toes. Some things were better shown in person. Her old boss at the tannery taught her a lot of commercial tanning tricks and the proper use of a fleshing machine. She began researching advanced tanning through the International School of Tanning Technology. She didn't actually take their amazing courses but rather printed their curriculum and began researching each topic mentioned individually. This was how Crystal found out about tanneries in Africa and all around the world! She applied for a position with the Solidaridad Network to help be a liaison to encourage the proper disposal of tanning wastes in tanneries. After all, she wasn't some environmental paper-pusher. She was a tanner and taxidermist. How often do you hear of an environmentalist/animal rights activist that is also a tanner/wildlife trapper/taxidermist? She had a beautiful blend that could offer a middle ground of understanding and respect.

Crystal-Dawn never got to see the tanneries, but she did get to see and smell the streets of Douala, where the gutters filled with all sorts of nastiness, impeding the flow of water. This was why she needed to go to Africa. If Solidaridad said, "Okay, we need you in Ethiopia, have you been before? Do you know of their circumstance?" She would need to say, "I have not been to Ethiopia, but I have been to Cameroon and know of their circumstance."

From the moment Crystal stepped off the airplane, she was instantly filled with panic from the smell that filled her nostrils, smoke. It was not the delightful campfire smoke she enjoyed or the burn barrels of the farm. This was a terrifying smell that signaled immediate danger. Another passenger she had previously chatted with in Paris was a concrete engineer that traveled there frequently for consultation reassured her there was no fire, and you get used to the smell.

She never did, not until the last day of her journey when something momentous happened that changed the smell and stirred the senses. She was in Yaoundé, Kribi, Douala, and Massambou in her few weeks there. She was traveling with her partner who was known as "America," for he had a greater understanding of English than French. He could also speak Pidgeon, his mother's tongue Douala and his father's tongue—*Something with a B*, she thought. Clearly a very intelligent man, he had trained as a computer programmer and dreamed of building a map app so that people could traverse the city as not all streets had names or numbers. Imagine trying to find a business with no address. He was trying to help his people through new digital technologies. Crystal-Dawn still had her outdoors Okanagan dream festering in her mind, needing completion, and Paul offered to help.

Although a completely common prole, her presence was greatly felt by others and was most definitely memorable! Crystal-Dawn represented

Canadians quite well. When the maid was dismissed for stealing her money, Crystal stepped up and helped wash floors and do laundry. Despite having done laundry by hand in her trailer's bathtub previously, she learned she was absolutely terrible at it, and it was for a fact that the people she encountered cared more for clean, beautiful white clothes than she did. She rolled in the red dirt and was almost always covered in a red haze, which was good because, for a Canadian in January, she was as white as she could ever be. Men constantly shouted out, "Femme blanche." It was odd because in Canada if you yelled out, "Hey, black man," you could be charged if the person saw fit to persecute you to the fullest extent of the law. Yet here, it was so common it became like a nickname for her. She didn't take offense. Only once did Paul react strongly to what someone had said to him about her, strongly enough to indicate a fight would occur.

Paul really stood up for himself and others in the community. He lived in an area that was difficult to drive cars into due to the condition of the roads. They were so roughly pitted out it was near impossible to drive through, yet some drivers were willing to risk their cars for a higher rate of pay. Most traveled by way of a motorcycle taxi. Those guys would remember Crystal. It was uncommon for passengers to hold onto the driver but rather sat back holding the sides of their seat with no helmets and no seat belts in cars. One time she saw a woman with her children catching a ride on a motorcycle. One child was placed in front of the driver with his arms around the child operating the bike. Behind him was another child squished between the man's back and his mother's chest. While most North Americans forget their seat belts or complain of the need for helmets with disdain, here was a population of people that didn't even have the choice to be safe and protect their lives and the lives of their children. Crystal was 100 percent positive it was impossible for her to cross a road in Yaoundé by herself without dying. Traffic, driving, transport, that whole area of necessity for a "civil" society to flourish was a complete safety nightmare. She feared for the life of every individual that ever needed to go near a road. There was also corruption in the process of applying for a driver's license where money and then more money would eventually free up a license for an individual. It was not based on driving ability although the reality of driving in Yaoundé was not something that could be taught. If it was, the lessons would be, go when you can, stop before you hit someone, then go when you can. Whenever, wherever, if you see an opening, you take it.

When she traveled in Kribi, an incident occurred that sent a shock wave through the whole city. They had been on the exact spot hours prior to the event. A large logging truck was driving through the city, and the logs loosened and crashed across the road. At least one woman died in Crystal's recollection. Yes, it was her birthday on January 26 because they were on the oceanfront with a Rasta man that owned a decrepit hotel he was fixing. That day a man came and joined them with great sadness in his heart. His family had died in the accident. Despite Crystal being from the only other French-English bilingual country in the world, she couldn't speak French. She knew the basic words to describe things, but it was not enough to hold a conversation. Also, Crystal typically spoke at lightning speeds, so it made it difficult for English-speaking Africans to follow. Her experiences were mostly from how the situations felt. When she was in the fish market on her birthday, a woman was making her some fresh prawns. There was a baby sleeping as she cooked, but it stirred and cried. Crystal was given the baby to soothe and cuddle while her food was being made. It was the best experience ever as she realized she could have stolen this woman's baby. That may sound odd so let's rephrase that by saying Crystal had been entrusted with the extended life force of another individual. That was truly a most wonderful sign of trust and love.

There were only a few moments where Crystal had truly felt fearful, and it was always in the presence of the police or some uniformed official. When traveling from one region to another by bus, all passengers must have an ID and be prepared for stops along the way where they check IDs. It was here that the proles were harassed, had their IDs held in return for payment, and barred travel. This happened several times on the journey, but one time was different. Paul was shouting at the man. He didn't have time to translate often while in the middle of speaking with someone, so often Crystal was left confused as to what was occurring. This time the man wanted them both to exit the bus at night. Paul refused as he had shown the IDs, and there was no just cause. He told her later that was how they got people. They had to separate themselves from others as extortion in public was dangerous because the people would rise up against them if pushed too far for an unjust cause.

In the Village of Massambou, his family owned a plantation. Palm trees and banana trees were the main crops. His family traveled between Yaoundé, Douala, and Massambou regularly to attend to matters at the plantation and court. They had once entrusted a man to watch their home in the village. When they returned, they learned he had sold all their furniture, pocketed the money, and disappeared. A lawyer in Douala was handling a long dispute over the plantation they owned in Massambou. When they originally divvied up the land into parcels, special trees were planted that grew high above the rest. You could stand in the jungle and see the corners of your property by locating these massive trees. We're talking dinosaur big. A famous football player had laid claim to their plantation and had a rich father backing him to legally sway the courts to steal this land from its rightful owners that farmed the land and give it to this football player. The courts were corrupt, but they did not give up. It was a regular occurrence to travel for court dates by bus. Aside from the legal battle, there was another problem felt more locally that the people of the village were divided as to whose side of the dispute they were on. Some preferred the football player and the money he brought to the village. Some loved the original owners that had deep ties and friendships with the elders of the community. There was one woman in her eighties cheerfully clearing the brush off her land in the jungle, amazing people.

A small creek came through the village that connected to a larger river with some larger predators Crystal didn't want to encounter, so she kept to the smaller creek. Although the travel agent had made it sound as though Crystal should not interact with the environment at all, she connected with Africa in every way possible. She swam and bathed in the creek. She also stepped on a broken iron cable in the creek, which left metal in her foot and became the "sole" excuse for not wanting to wear shoes. It was easy to skip barefoot on the red dusty paths of roads, villages, and cities; however, the jungle was a different story. There were many pokey plants in the jungle that caused one's feet to beg for shoes. The vines were amazing and not at all what Tarzan had made them out to be.

The people. The people of the village were curious about this femme blanche skipping about and one evening began to gather outside the family home at dinner. Crystal hadn't even noticed the group forming outside the window. His father approached the window and told Paul to take Crystal away from view and hide her. She was placed in her room as the family dealt with the situation brewing outside. She was told they were fearful the villagers may cause an issue. There were a lot of rising tensions, and her presence could cause a feud. After legal issues were handled in Douala, they were back on a bus to Yaoundé. She loved the bus rides. They were hot and crowded with no option for a bathroom. Can you imagine trying to hold it until the next planned stop? It was not easy. She sang her entire mental album of Simon & Garfunkle out loud. It was epic.

Back in Yaoundé, she toured the zoo and met friends, family, neighbors, business owners, and anyone that would smile in exchange.

She climbed trees and skipped down roads. Her new mother-in-law and sisters even braided her hair. It was gorgeous. On the last day of her time in Africa, something happened. In Africa the seasons were different than in North America. It is either hot or rainy. It had been hot and muggy throughout the entire trip to the point of not being able to wear makeup as it would just sweat off. On the last day, they traveled to visit a concrete artist. He had a business of finishing the exterior of buildings and fences in such a way it looked like carved natural wood. Crystal learned a lot of concrete work as it turned out they didn't plan ahead for the weather. Rain or sun, they poured the concrete and did the work required of them. She was no expert but knew the temperature of concrete curing affected the result, so she found it rather silly there was no planning around the weather. Regardless, it was the dry season. It would not rain.

After a wonderful visit, they parted ways. Exiting the building, the sky was not yet visible, yet the world felt so completely different it was as though a whole new energy filled the air. It was as shocking as the smell of smoke in one's nose upon first smelling Africa. As they walked further into the street, the buildings opened revealing a darkened sky. It was going to rain. She felt it. Within the next five to ten minutes, storm clouds rolled in that began a rainstorm that felt like a monsoon. Crystal was supposed to be flying home that evening, so Paul left her at the house to fetch a car. She spent her last few hours dancing in the rain. The ride arrived what could be perceived as late, but they had an hour to travel to the airport. The roads were full of vehicles, and traffic moved so slowly from the storm. It was feared they would not arrive in time. There was very little communication between Crystal and Paul and his parents who had joined to drop her off. He wore her winter camouflage jacket as they drove. She needed it as it was now February when she would arrive back in Canada. News of Covid and potential travel lockdowns were imminent. The taxi arrived at such a time that they ran into the airport to get in the line. She was a little late for their security clearing time but had not missed the flight. She was taken to an office where a kind-faced woman gave her no answers as to what would happen with her flight. Could she catch it, could she rebook? Her family was waiting at both airports for her to drop her off and pick her up, and she needed to tell the news. A security man was consulted and gave no answers Crystal could understand. Crystal saw Paul waving to her from across the gates so she requested he be present to translate because she could not understand what was being spoken. He was permitted access and after many, many words, he said she could go. She gave quick goodbye hugs and threw on her jacket for the trip that lay before her on the journey home. She asked later what had happened in the airport, and he told her the guard was trying to extort money from her, but she was too naïve to know it. Apparently, most people in that situation would have offered money to make the flight happen. Rather, Paul had shouted publicly across the airport that this man was corrupt. That was Paul, standing up for what was right.

Their romance ended when he tried to take his life. It was a sad story that showed life was hard enough, but life in Africa was mostly survival.

J' aimerais vivre dans tes chaussures pour être avec toi à chacun de tes pas.

I told you I wanted to live in your shoes so I could be with you every step of the way.
You told me your shoes were mine.
I believed you.
I believed in you.
So you tucked me in close to your heart and continued walking on your way.

Oh, how fickle relationships can be.
You had a disagreement.
I thought you forgot you still had me close to your heart when you decided to take a stroll through hell.

I thought my last words would be I love you.
Rather I'm haunted by, "Why did you do this?"
A selfish desire for logic in an unimaginable moment.

How was I to save you?
All I could do was make a call and wait in that hell you left me in.
Wait as I heard the door smash in and hear the screams of every person that walked into that hell echo off the concrete walls.
And then the phone went dead, leaving me in that hell alone with the screams resonating through the silence.

You were saved. They got to you in time.
Time. How fickle time can be.
It can literally build a path out of hell,

Creating a physical distance from the freshness of the most painful memories.

In time I will find my way out of this hell.

I pray these scars do not mar me but remind me of the pain we have the ability to inflict on those around us. We are not alone. Whether or not you are physically alone right now, you are never alone and your actions can create a ripple affecting many lives.

He had been attacked after Crystal left Africa. Men thought he had money since he had been seen with a white woman. He fended off a lot of men, but they hurt him. This was just weeks after having recently taken an ax blow to the head. He needed a good woman that could bear children anyway, and Crystal couldn't do that. He hadn't had that life experience yet and really deserved it. He would be an amazing father one day. It is only hoped he meets a woman worthy of his heart. Crystal-Dawn learned she could speak to the French Cameroonians through song. She couldn't speak French, but she could sing it.

> Frère Jacques, Frère Jacques,
> Dormez-vous? Dormez-vous?
> Sonnez les matines, sonnez les matines
> Ding, ding, dong, ding, ding, dong.

It was already 5:00 p.m. on a Thursday evening. Crystal reflected that meant she had been writing this book for at least a week now because it was the night of the pool league at the Army Navy. She wrote out a summary of her plans for the president and dropped it off after picking up her daughter from school. The president wished to speak with her, but she was required to wear shoes. After a quick search of the truck, she found some gum boots to throw on and began the meeting. He was grumpy. He folded her request in half and said he had no interest in murals, snacks, landscaping, or any of it. The agenda was now down to just the pool tournament. They could play this evening.

10:00 p.m.—it was nearing the time for rest when Crystal was finally able to revisit her story. It was time for bed, and she needed a bath and readied herself. She had spent the last few hours keeping score, reading the Bible and the *New Business Guide* by Hansford. The title was somewhat illegible on the cover and some pages rat chewed, but this book contained all knowledge needed in the dominion of Canada in 1892 (perhaps). This book will come up again in the future as it held the key basic principles of a civilized society. Today had reached its end though, and balance of all things required rest. Tomorrow she would try to write about the parallel universe realities and how the animals used this to change the future for all.

May 13, 2022

Chapter 5

The fruitage of the spirit was a teaching of the Christian religion. It could not be stopped by the machine, but it could be twisted and sometimes changed with cause. The fruitage was love, joy, peace, long-suffering, gentleness, goodness, faith, meekness, and temperance. These were altered to become love, joy, peace, long-suffering, kindness, goodness, faith, mildness, and self-control. Eventually long-suffering was changed to patience. Regardless of the terminology used, the machine took this fruit and fermented it and fed it back to the animals as truth. They were drunk on the idea of these qualities without ever having to actually act this way in their day-to-day lives. The kind of nice words that when one spoke of them, others placated them, saying, "That's nice, dear."

The animals needed to get off the fermented fruits so they could create a mutual reality. The problem was the animals had so many alternate realities occurring within the same world. It had fractured them apart. They could not connect to each other being in such alternate realities, for instance, the elephants. The true reality was that elephants were factually large, peace-loving herbivores. This was a fact of nature. However, over time, with the thoughts of men poisoning their minds, some of the animals began to perceive the elephants as dangerous, terrifying beasts that must be killed for the safety of all the other animals. Some animals focused on the mighty elephants' tusks and saw a financial gain. Surely if they possessed the tusks of the mighty elephant, they too would be mighty. It was this fracture of reality in the minds of the animals that made peace seem impossible.

The animals of the world needed to align their chakras and clear their minds of all the fractured realities that existed within. The crystal was able to assist with this as the crystal was a real object the animals could see. Totems and gems were not meant to be worshipped but merely representative of something that was not a physical object. Some animals had strong enough minds they didn't need totems. They could perfectly see what was occurring within themselves and the world. With their minds cleared of the thoughts of men, they were ready to see the world for what it truly was.

It was the awakening of the animals.

Some cried over the state of Mother Earth. That was why they hadn't wanted to think about it. It was terrible.

Some cried over the state of the other animals. They hadn't known how bad it was, or they had an inclination but didn't want to think about it.

Some cried over the state of the lesser species and how the animals had used and abused them.

Some cried over the poisoned water; some cried over the poisoned food.

Enough tears were cried by all the animals it cleaned the earth of the filth that the machine had created over the years.

They became hopeful and began to focus on the heart that needed starting for it could not rely on the over-crazed, forced pumping of the machine for much longer. This is where the healing vibrational frequencies were necessary.

The doves long held the secrets of the healing vibrations. The Egyptians had known about it and hid the secrets within the Great Pyramids. It was known that the most loved book, the Bible, had been altered by the thoughts of men. It was difficult of course to discern upon a study where the changes had occurred. If anyone dared suggest an entry was made that would stifle animals from finding the truth within the text, it was suggested they were trying to place animals before God. Religion had long been used by the machine to its advantage. Like the PDDs, it was not the machine's invention but rather used by the machine to divide the animals. They had to look within their true beliefs to find the Word of God and the thoughts of men. All throughout the world, hints of truth were left for the animals, not within one organization, religion, place, or object, but many. Each of these hints had been tainted by the thoughts of men and had to be studied. Many religions taught crystals, stones, or gems were divinations and surely the work of the devil even though the Old Testament spoke of their use with holy individuals.

The doves' key was the healing vibrations, and these healed the animals' bodies and souls.

Music rang throughout the Earth and created a vibrational wave frequency that touched every chakra throughout the animals. Some referred to this feeling as being filled with Holy Spirit. It is an amazing feeling that can be felt within a large group of people vibrating on the same frequency. It is a force more powerful than the strongest static electricity you've ever felt. The animals did have power when they worked together, not just physically but mentally. They began loving one another freely without fear their neighbor would hurt them. The animals opened their hearts to each other. They apologized for their wrongdoings and began doing everything in their power to right the wrongs they had committed:

> to each other
> to the Earth
> to the lesser species

The Earth's heart began glowing green and slowly a vibrational pulse was felt throughout the Earth. Again, it pulsed and again grew in strength and might. The team of animal specialists of every kind began surgical work on the heart as they now had Faith she would survive the surgery. Tumors of every kind were removed. How long it took was unknown as the tumors had greatly integrated themselves right into the bloodstream. Filters were put in place to clean the Earth's water as it pumped through her to renew her and flush out the poisons. All the unnecessary bureaucratic tumors were removed, and a strong foundation of roots from the Tree of Life grew around the heart, protecting it for all time.

Seven roots encased the strong green glowing heart.

One root represented the governing body for the Earth, its soil, and coverings, the mother's flesh and skin.

One root represented the governing body for the water, the mother's blood, and the fountain of life for all species.

One root represented the governing body for the science of the Earth; they would use science to create laws that could be enforced globally to protect Mother Earth.

One root represented the governing body for indigenous peoples; they would represent the heritage and history of a time that could never be forgotten and must always be remembered and learned from so such mistakes never happened again.

One root represented the governing body for wildlife; they would represent all species of Earth that needed to always be considered forever into the future.

One root represented the governing body for the animals; each community would send their wisest and most selfless representative that had given the most to their community and cared the most for others.

One root represented the governing body of truth to guide animalkind toward the future of their choosing. Planning for the future was not a one-time occurrence in the history of the world, and future generations needed an opportunity to build upon the foundation that these animals laid for them.

The Self-Authoring of Animalkind

Chickens were abundant throughout the Earth and known well for their clucking but not the meaning of their message of "truth". The chickens actually held the secret bestowed upon them through God, of how an organization made by animals should be properly run to put the truth of God first before all else. Their communities were congregations of adequate size, so the members were cared for and didn't fall between the cracks with no tithes. If someone gave so much of themselves holding a full-time position within the organization and couldn't hold full-time employment, they were given a modest wage to live on to continue their efforts. The congregation was headed by elders, the wise, older ones. They were at the center.

What the chickens knew was as simple as geometry. The old world of men had been organized as a triangle as seen with the pyramids. Perfect triangles only existed within the smallest of the world's creations. Crystals could form them, but they were not typical. Circles were typical. The Earth, the rounded stones of the rivers washed and tumbled by the cleaning effects of water. Amazing, isn't it? When a stone is subjected to water and grit, it removes abrasive edges and polishes it to a perfect circle. The animals needed grit, but it was deemed dirty.

That was how the chickens organized themselves. In loving circles, similar to that of a flock of sheep. The old world of men, before the days of the Egyptians, worshipped power, not God. The power of a triangle offered a few to rise to the top on the backs of others. Some admired the Great Pyramids and marveled at their beauty in the sun of the desert. What an amazing feat of engineering so great, it must be of another world, for their technologies could not have created such perfection! The fractured realities of the past had shown some men a different view upon sight of the Great Pyramids. They saw the blood-soaked sand, and corpses crying out from under the foundations but they did not care. They saw a means to attain power, a means to be above all else in their towers of power. They admired the pharaoh's efforts and cared not for the thousands that died, giving their energy and life to the pyramid. These were the men that created the machine based on the principles of the Great Pyramids. The animals were even aware of it. They called it a pyramid scheme and recognized the whole world was built on this principle of a triangle with the masses at the bottom elevating the powerful few. In reality, there was no room for one single individual to be at the top as it was a point and had no room for one individual to rule all. One would continually try to rise to the top and fall off, so it was well known no one could rule, but all could strive to be as near the top as possible to feel the power of the sun's energy.

The chicken's circle, once known, was globally admired and became the new system of the world. At the center of a community were the wise elders, who throughout their lives had been most selfless, giving of themselves to those in the community. They were the most admired. They had a positive energy to radiate outward to all animals, just as the sun radiates energy to the Earth. Those strongest in faith and hope for animalkind strived to be near the center of the energy. If an animal worked really, really hard, it could earn peace and security near the center of its power. They became eternal in the collective reality of the memory of the animals. No animal actually wanted to live forever. They just wanted a good life during their time on Earth. It had a good meaning, happy, peaceful, loved, cared for, successful in their endeavors, positively challenging, fun, and exciting. They wanted to grow and experience all life and the world had to offer without the thoughts of men. Fear, anger, hurt, jealousy, greed, and gluttony were memories of the past. Every tear was wiped from the animals' eyes, and they cried no more. They had used God's love and the lessons taught from the sacrifice of so many great renegades to begin creating the future of their choosing, for the betterment of all.

A wise owl had been helping the animals self-author their own lives. He taught the animals they needed to learn from their past and heal. They needed to consider the animal they were in the present, so they could draw on their strengths and recognize their weaknesses. Not one animal was perfect, but together they strengthened each other by helping teach one another with loving-kindness. Then they needed to plan their future. Where did they want to be in a few years? Then imagine, what was the worst-case scenario that could happen. They took that fear and put it behind them as something to be avoided and to stay the "hell" away from. See that? The animals admitted there was a hell, and they didn't want to experience it. They decided what their personal heaven was and worked hard daily to create it in the world around them. When all the animals worked together toward a globally accepted goal, progress was exponential.

12:30 p.m.

Gerrasimos was gone for the day helping his parents do tasks around their home and then fixing his mom's car with his brother. She had the day to write alone with all the kids safely in school. Her phone was still broken, but she had email contact and was able to borrow Gerrasimos or the girls' phone when necessary for phone calls. She had been trying to contact the Human Rights Watch to find out what could be done to protect her family in Cameroon before the book was published. It was nearing its end, and she would soon need to send that email to an agent, and then the rain would begin. Last night had been a terrible storm. Rain pounding on a Quonset metal roof is magnified. Crystal loved living in a shop and dreamed of opening her bedroom door, coffee magically already in hand, standing overlooking her workshop below. A renovated barn would be amazing with living space above and a workshop below. For now, they were in this shop, and this shop was a small old house with many additions, a relic of the past existing between two new cinderblock buildings. It was a great location on what she would consider to be perhaps the third main road running north to south through Vernon. It was the road people took to avoid the highway and secondary main road. It also had a large walking path that allowed for safe travel for pedestrians and cyclists. With the new electric scooters available on every corner to rent, this spot offered interesting sights. Crystal-Dawn loved sitting outside, watching everything. Pondering could not occur indoors as thoughts became trapped, but outdoors she could connect to the world. So many fantastic porch ponderings have occurred throughout time just by sitting with nature and pondering. Those who seek the truth will have it revealed to them. This was promised. Between the Bible, the 1889 book of business, The *People's Home Library of 1915* and George Orwell, and endless shows every night of every learning topic on curiosity stream, Crystal-Dawn had truly been given answers to every question she sought.

Just this morning before Gerrasimos left, they had had another uncomfortable morning. Once again, she had mentioned throughout the show as they drifted to sleep that she felt like she couldn't talk to him because she had something she needed to say but could not find the right words because every combination of words to express that thought had been said before, and she already knew where that conversation led. She wanted to know when was he going to make time for her. Now this was of course as mentioned a sensitive topic. I will not waste time with emotions and feelings but rather on facts. They had busy lives. Between running their two businesses, three children full time, and three usually on weekends but now apparently not for weeks on end with no mention of communication other than a mediator which was good, they needed to get something in writing, but it was made apparent no one actually enforces it if the parent refuses visitation. Crystal had a friend in the US named Jacob. He had recently made the most soulful post describing his pain in not seeing his two children in two years I believe it was. She just refused. The children in the picture must have been perhaps four and six. They were young, too young to be able to demand to see their father or understand the truth as to why they hadn't seen him in so long. Some people did not experience that feeling as a child and could not understand these situations. Crystal-Dawn had lived so many lives she could relate to many things. When she was perhaps eight, she decided she no longer wanted to see her father. One night, in front of their home in Calgary on the front steps, her aunt, her father's own sister, told her a story of her father from the past that made Crystal decide in her child-sized mind that her father was a BAD man. In the story, her father had lived in Ontario, which may have been Toronto specifically, but there were so many suburbs it was hard to say for certain. He had encountered a young boy on the street with a pet raccoon. Allegedly he offered to buy the raccoon and the boy said no, so he took the raccoon.

    She missed out on every weekend visitation with him for a year before they were swept away to British Columbia because of a child's sense of righteousness that it was wrong to take a raccoon from a kid. Her mother never talked sense into her, granted there were also memories of times he would stand outside the house in the dark yelling at her mother. In the end, neither were saints. He was the kind of man that admired the Japanese and wanted an obedient woman. She just wanted to draw close to Jehovah and live a good life, studying his word and spreading the good news of the kingdom. He figured her faith meant she could never leave him. He straight up said that. He was an interesting man that lived in a miserable history that he struggled to get past. His parents were cruel, the foster homes were hard, and he was alone, had two kids and they were taken by their mom. He got married and had two more and lost them. The biggest point of contention was the bloody house. "A man's home is his castle," he would say. Can you imagine weekend visitation with your dad and he drives past your old house every time telling you the current value and how much money they would have had if she hadn't left him? My goodness, there were times he even tried to complain about their sexual life because apparently certain acts were not allowed. He was in his twenties during the 1970s and nonreligious, so sexual stuff was no issue. One weekend on a road trip, they discovered a hitchhiker's bag on the side of the road, full of porn. They were old porn with bush. It was actually quite kind of her father to let her sit silently in the back gaping at these images while he and her brother conversed in the front.

Ah sexuality, have we made our way back there? Delightful! In 1984 it is explained that sex had been perverted in the mind of women. It was a shameful, dirty act committed by those who lived in filth and sin with no self-control. Oh my goodness, it's time! There is a song. This song was Crystal's mantra throughout her first nineteen years. It was how she drew close to God. The original existed in a few minds and cannot be published in the entirety for copyright infringements so here's the five never-forgotten verses:

> #191 Make the Truth Your Own
> By putting God first, and Him actively praising, this world and its friendship you'll lose.
> To those without faith, it is truly amazing that God's righteous ways you did then choose!
> Make the Truth your own.
> Shun the world, leave it alone.
> if your body members you control, you make known that the truth is your own.

That's right. The congregations used to sing praises to Jehovah for controlling their bodies' members. Masturbation. Sself-abuse, I believe was the old term. There are people who believe it is impossible for an individual to not masturbate, and it is guaranteed that there are indeed people in our world that receive absolutely no pleasure from their own touch. There were many things that had changed over time. That was evident in Crystal's history books.

- Hallelujah is wrong. It's actually, alleluia.

If you're going to sing praises, use the right words. AD 1611 Bible says so.

- God's name is Jehovah or Yahweh in Hebrew.

Fact, if you're going to talk to the God of the Bible, try to get to know Him. He has a name.

- The word matrix used to mean womb

Now something like an intercellular matrix is a fine webbing of simple cells. One does not imagine a womb when thinking of the word matrix.

- 1 tablespoon was equivalent to 4 teaspoons

Just as 2 + 2 = 5 because someone said it was so, so over time we all came to know it to be so.

The world of 2022 was one that was made by men with power and money being its chief concerns. Even the original ideals of mankind were lost in the generations.

It was once taught to the generation of 1889, "Young men, you are architects of your own fortunes. Rely upon your own strength of body and soul. Take for your star, self-reliance. Don't take too much advice—keep at your helm and steer your own ship, and remember that the great art of commanding is to take a fair share of the work. Think well of yourself. Strike out. Assume your own position. Put potatoes in a cart over rough road, and the small ones go to the bottom. Rise above the envious and jealous. Fire above the mark you intend to hit. Energy invincible determination, with a right motive, are the levers that move the world. Be in earnest. Be self-reliant. Be generous. Be civil. Read the papers. Advertise your business. Make money, and do good with it. Love your God and fellowmen. Love truth and virtue. Love your country and obey its laws" (J. L. Nichols, *The Business Guide or Safe Methods of Business*).

This book contains some of the wisest words ever written for people, all people. While terribly outdated as Canada was not even an independent country yet, this book was all that a person needed to go out into the world and be a good person, not only surviving but thriving.

The Peoples Home Library was a massive book with a collection of three books. These are *The Peoples Home Medical Book* by T. J. Ritter, *The Peoples Home Recipe Book* by Alice G. Kirk, and *The Peoples Home Stock Book* by W. C. Fair.

With the third book being the most original Bible of 1611 that could be gotten, these three books contained all the knowledge required for an individual. She hoped her children would see the importance of such books for more than just their age and cool random facts their mother spouted from time to time in her readings.

The movie *The Book of Eli* demonstrated the value of the knowledge held within books if ever a time occurred when we are without the means of power we now are reliant on. It was a little surprising the book he held was a Bible but made sense that the bad guy would want a book of power. A practical, "normal" person would rather have hoped to attain a book of farming to grow food or perhaps a book of medical advice and natural medicine. These would be the books of true value to a person. Those books offered physical care while the Bible offered mental and emotional care.

It had occurred to Crystal reading the Bible during the game of pool, that the Songs of Psalms were the kind of words she had in her head for her partner Gerrasimos. They were the loving words of Celine

Dion because he was her reason to get out of bed and sleep through the night. She did adore him and most definitely always wanted to floor him. The sweet words of Paul Simon rang through her head, in her imagination:

> I hear the drizzle of the rain; like a memory it falls, soft and warm continuing, tapping on my roof and walls.
>
> And from the shelter of my mind, through the window of my eyes, I gaze beyond the rain-drenched streets, to England where my heart lies.
>
> My mind's distracted and diffused; my thoughts are many miles away.
>
> They lie with you when you're asleep, and kiss you when you start your day.
>
> And a song I was writing is left undone; I don't know why I spend my time, writing songs I can't believe, with words that tear and strain to rhyme.
>
> And so you see I have come to doubt; all that I once held as true.
>
> I stand alone without beliefs; the only truth I know is you.
>
> (Simon & Garfunkle, "Kathy's Song")

That's how Crystal-Dawn felt about Gerrasimos. This is how she wanted him to think of her:

> What I dream I had, pressed in organdy, clothed in crinoline of smoky Burgundy, softer than the rain.

I wandered empty streets, past the shop displays down,
I heard cathedral bells.

Tripping down the alleyways as I walked on, and when you ran to me, your cheeks flushed with the night.

We walked on frosted fields, of juniper and lamplight;
I held your hand.

And when I awoke and felt you warm and near, I kissed your honey hair with my grateful tears.

Oh, I love you, girl

Oh, I love you!

(Simon & Garfunkle, "For Emily, Wherever I May Find Her")

    See Crystal-Dawn had a dreamy, poetic mind that felt great emotions typically experienced by those who have open heart chakras. They wear their heart on their sleeve and experience all that life has to offer, offering love to all, used by some, unappreciated by many. Some went so far as to call it a mental illness and mediated those who felt too strongly. Surely it was easier to medicate them than to learn what was occurring and why. How could someone possibly understand why if they don't even ask? Emotions were not bad. They are the foundation of reason because they tell us what to value. Crystal-Dawn was once told she must be on lithium. She only knew this word in conjunction with batteries and thought it an amusing idea someone thought she was energized with battery power.
    It's not what they meant. Apparently, lithium is also an antidepressant of some sort.
    Crystal had tried medication a few times, years back. It was terrible. Perhaps it was necessary at that time to stop the crying, but once the hysteria ended, it just made her sleep. She would literally fall asleep at

the city playground with her four-year-old waiting for school to let out. That was not OK. Then her eldest won a bicycle at school. She couldn't even fake enthusiasm for such a wonderful thing to occur. She was numb, a numb shell that spent four hours a day taking public transport to get the children to and from school and daycare and sat in therapy classes or appointments in between. Months of life were spent getting well, learning communication skills, gaining strength, and learning the physical and mental problems related to eating disorders and mental illness. Group therapy classes were wonderful and showed the amazing variety of people struggling in our world every day with something as simple as eating food.

Food was life-sustaining. Why was there such a problem with something that is necessary to preserve life? Crystal appreciated food but strongly disliked it. She didn't like physical necessities. It sounded childish but she preferred to do something because she wanted to by choice and not due to a forced physical urge of necessity.

It was much like one would wish to have bladder control so as to not piss oneself randomly when the urge was present. Crystal preferred to eat when it was convenient to do so and would not have her physical form impede what needed to be done. Everything else came first—the children, the cleaning, the work, everything. There were so many layers of complexity as to why Crystal didn't like food at least not until after 4:00 p.m. or 5:00 p.m. preferably, but that would be a book of its own. Regardless it was deemed as disordered eating and when control was lost, no food entered her body, so it was quite detrimental to her health at times. Whether eating too much or too little, no extreme has ever been good as there was balance required in all things.

Chapter 6

The owl joined the governing bodies, and a system was created so each animal had a vote. Systematically, all the animals addressed independent issues. The leaders gladly handed over the crown. The leaders had studied history as well and knew the power was temporary and fleeting, and at any time in the future, the past could be rewritten, making them monsters and telling of their monstrous ways. Or they could take the easy way out and receive praise from animals around the world and be remembered as being the last great leader of that country, and no matter how treacherous their reign had been, they were a hero forever for voluntarily handing over the crown for the greater good of all animals, the Earth, and all other species. Everyone thought it would take a revolution of guns when really it was a revolution of thought. They began to educate themselves on the ways of the world—food, politics, and the environment. All the important matters of the world were being learned by all and shared in conversation. The animals were delighted for this conversation truly fed their souls. They craved being heard and having their opinion valued. It was worth learning about these topics now because they no longer brought sadness as topics that nothing could be done about. The animals' minds were freed from the thoughts of men, so they could create their own ideas. Their ideas mattered because each and every animal had a vote on all major issues that needed resolving.

Ideas became the new highly valued commodity. Thinkers who were creative and could create solutions were quite valuable globally.

They became the superstars that most animals aspired to. Nikola Tesla was honored as the ancient superstar that created the last burst of energy the world needed. He spent his life working for the betterment of animalkind and could have elevated the entire animal race. No longer would good, creative individuals be stifled, extorted, or used by a capitalist world seeking financial gain and power. Those were the thoughts of men, and they were the hell that the animals strived to stay away from. They didn't want to be angry. It didn't feel good. They didn't want to be jealous of the other animals. They wanted to love themselves and be someone they could be proud of. Amazing animals were not something to be jealous of; they were wonderful examples of how to be, so the other animals could follow their lead. Gluttony was deemed an unnecessary, unhealthy lack of self-control, and those with strong urges were given help.

The prisons of the future would amuse those with memories of the Old World. You see, all animals were inherently good by nature. It just so happened that with all things, a balance was required. The world still contained predators, and they needed a place. It was not unnatural for a shark to eat a dolphin, no matter how devastating or painful it is to that particular dolphin and its family and community. Despite being predators, sharks needed love and appreciation too.

When the world changed its structure to circular, the predators were no longer at the top of a pyramid food chain. The people organized themselves like a flock of sheep with the predators on the outside. It was recognized that it was natural for them to want to hunt and be free, so a place was made for them at the edge of the flock. Rather than being a wolf that preyed upon the flock, they could be a guardian and protect the flock.

Almost all the wolves leaped at the opportunity. They could do what they wanted to do and be honored for it. The guardians that protected the flock were of course free to roam within the flock and were given an annual celebration. A feast was created for them by all the herbivores that were so grateful the wolves decided to change their ways, just enough to not eat them any longer. There were always going to be wolves with a taste for blood and even sheep that bickered and bit one another occasionally, but the guardians kept peace and order.

Another small change that created a ripple throughout future generations was also a construct of the chickens, that the children not be separated from the adults. The machine had been taking children from morning until night and sometimes indefinitely and indoctrinating the children on how to be successful cogs in its machine. The machine needed energy, and the children were the future energy source to pay its debt. That was seen as archaic and education advanced. The entire upbringing of children in developed countries balanced with that of the undeveloped countries. The children needed to learn the skills required for life, and these were seldom taught in schools. There had been such an overabundance of information; the fundamentals were lost. Parents had been too busy supplying energy to the machine to give any to their children. Some parents should never have been parents to begin with as they never had any intentions of giving their children any of their energy. They merely paid for their children's existence and in later years upon reflection saw it as a huge lump sum of money that could have advanced their own lives rather than that of a child they never heard from anymore.

The new system not only allowed children in the workplace, but it encouraged it. Children became members of the community and were responsible for it. All the animals marveled when a new child joined the community and participated in its growth. Animals were no longer devastated when they lost a loved one because there were so many animals in their life to love and remember.

There became three planes of existence the animals became aware of.

The present—it was within their immediate field of vision. The other animals, the plants, the movements, and experiences at the moment.

The mountains—those who lived in regions with no mountains looked to the line of the horizon. These mountains represented the immediate future. For in those mountains, at the present moment, many things were occurring. Other animals were scurrying about their business, plants were growing, etc. That also occurred in the present but was far away, so if the animals wished to be there and join those

animals, it became a hope, dream, or plan for the future. If it was a positive hope, such as to visit a friend or perhaps roll down the fluffy smooth hillsides, the mountains became a positive hopeful future to gaze upon in the present. One day, they would do that.

The sky—the sky filled all the space that existed above. Whether it be star gazing, finding shapes in clouds, praying to a higher power, or casting thoughts into the universe, it was globally recognized as a means for the animals to see beyond the actual present and planned future to something higher and greater.

Religious people were no longer persecuted. As long as everyone was following the laws the animals agreed upon, everyone was free to believe as they choose. No one wanted to be judged, so they stopped judging others. The animals became more clear in their communication with each other and tried their utmost to speak from a loving place in their hearts. Sometimes a beaver would drop a tree that an owl had been occupying, so they communicated and compromised which trees could and could not be cut for the betterment of all in the community and for the land herself. Had the beaver considered the water needed downstream before he began his dam? It was natural for the animals to not consider all the facts prior to taking action, but as long as they recognized the damage of their actions and sought to repair all damages to others, it was settled and over time all together avoided with new laws that required no lawyers.

The chickens opened their doors seeing this change and decided that yes, God had brought this new system through His Word, and especially since the new world was structured after their organization, they stopped knocking on the other animals' doors!

All the animals rejoiced on Saturday mornings when they no longer heard the clucking of hens or the crowing of roosters. It was so peaceful!

Crystal-Dawn laughed. If that wasn't enough to convince the people of the world. She didn't know what would work! It was true though! If the Jehovah's Witness governing body could be convinced that the end was not a bloody battle physically at our feet slaying the wicked but rather a battle of thought.

George Orwell said, "We do not merely destroy our enemies; we change them."

The people of the world were not inherently bad.

A common thread united mankind.

Food, water, shelter, space, and Love, are all we really need to ensure our physical needs are met so we can tame the flight-or-fight response when it is unnecessary.
It is the earth element within us.
It also influences our passion, creativity, youthfulness, and vitality. How could one unlock those without their basic needs being met?
It shows a need for logic, realistic thinking, and order in our lives.
We cannot connect with others if our basic needs are not met.

Next is the water element within us.
It impacts our ability to be happy and joyful, compassionate, creative, and passionate. It also influences our desires, sexuality, and our reproductive functions among others.
We cannot connect with others if we are blocking our true selves.

Next is fire, a fiery, powerful element of energy, when balanced, it allows us to be much more energetic, active, confident, and forthcoming.
Without it, we are unbalanced and cannot connect with others.

Next are the air elements within us.
This is our heart, Anahata.
Much like the water bearer Aquarius, the air element has little effect alone and requires another element to be powerful so too our hearts need other hearts to connect to be powerful.
Without an open heart, we cannot connect with others

Next is your throat, your true inner voice.
It aids in listening, empathizing, and communicating with others.
Without an open throat, we cannot freely communicate with others.

Next is your brow or frontal lobe.

This is where we conceive our sense of thought, our ability to rationalize, use logic, and conduct an analysis to reach reasonable conclusions.

Telepathic abilities are being able to read one's mind or convey thoughts without words.

When you're connected to someone and learn of their thoughts and habits, you learn how their mind thinks. In doing so, quite often you can anticipate the thoughts of that individual. It was quite a common practice.

Your thoughts were full of the thoughts of another thereby reaching the same conclusions. There is much more to it of course, but that is the simplified version of the known and accepted powers of the crown chakra's telepathic abilities.

There is so much more outside of an individual, which is where it really gets fun connecting with others. The more individuals balance their personal lives and open all their chakras, the more connected of a world we will become. The future was bright for mankind if they were willing to step outside in the rain and look at the world for the shared true, non-fractured reality it was. Because it needed every single person to BELIEVE, it was possible before it actually became possible. People could do anything, and they knew it. They just felt powerless to do anything about it.

Hope Lies with the Proles

Crystal-Dawn's totem was an ebony statue of a human holding a large boulder high above its head with an arched neck and back and with the left leg straight and right bent forward. Crystal literally used unicorn spit to add the colors of the chakras. After keeping this object about, it became clear to Crystal what it really was. This would signify her. Just as a voodoo doll could represent a person, so too this African statue could represent herself. She would think of this as both herself and an African woman, for she would never treat another person the way she treated herself. She was very unkind to herself.

You see she couldn't get pregnant anymore, so she couldn't quit smoking for the reason of doing it for the life of another. She ate just enough to survive as she clearly lived and breathed in the process of writing this book. However, she did not care for herself. Although she had worked hard to be a person she could be proud of through action and thoughts, her body was a burden.

People saw an attractive woman. Attractive women are expected to fit into specific molds, which clearly Crystal did not. She had an old man inside her or several perhaps. How she came to find a passion for taxidermy and trapping is a mystery. Reasons could be made of course. She thought Canada had a boring history, but it wasn't until trying it for herself she found how exciting it must have been pioneering the wilderness of British Columbia, not to mention challenging, cold, dangerous, and can you imagine the mosquitos? Anyway, people hadn't always treated Crystal the way a person ought to be treated. It made her not like her physical self very much because those people didn't actually know her, so they were not insulting, hurting, or hating the person she was. They were insulting, hurting, and hating whatever their perception was of her without having gotten to know her. They were hating the cover of her personal book. She didn't know why. You never truly know why someone is full of hate. Perhaps they don't even know. They have decided with pure ignorance they did not want to know anything about her, let alone the truth of her story.

7:00 p.m.

Gerrasimos was home and sitting with one of the children in Crystal's healing room, giving him a fairy tarot reading. They were both able to feel a tingle in their finger at a card, but Crystal could not. She always let someone else pick, and it was always bang on, sometimes frustratingly so. Crystal-Dawn stopped writing to lie on Gerrasimos and hear his reading—past, present, and future.

The Past Was Judgment

He looked over and noticed Crystal was wearing his underwear on her head. She said, "Don't judge. This card was perfectly timed."

The card read, "When you face the faerie of judgment, it is time to look carefully at your life and the possibilities before you. There is something you should be doing, something that would be a significant change from what you are doing. Whatever this something is, it is for the benefit of the universe and is essential to your spiritual growth. To hear your guidance clearly, open your heart and mind and be willing to accept the message."

The Present was the two of swords

The card read—you face a choice. You are in a situation or relationship or involved in a project that is requiring too much of your time and energy. Your life may become unbalanced as you neglect other responsibilities. Any situation that compels you to keep secrets from those you love is dangerous and unhealthy. Be honest with yourself about what you are doing and why. Making the right choice now could eliminate bigger problems or even tragedy later.

The future was the six of cups

The card read—something or someone is missing from your life, and you feel that loss quite deeply. You find a sort of peace in the past. Memories are funny things and are easily altered by time and distance. They can be bewitching and invasive. They can even be tyrants. Reliving memories can be comforting but don't let them keep you from living in the present.

Her daughter asked the deck what she should do with her future and joked about being a prostitute. Crystal suggested she try stripping before jumping straight in bed. It was a solid joke. She drew the devil card, irony.

Chapter 7

This portion of the book is more of a prelude to the full Self-Authoring of Animalkind book. The book contains the writings of more than one hundred authors of the renegades of the past, the great thinkers of the present, and space for growth for all future authors willing to step up on a global scale and help the world. Those are the animals who became immortal in the minds of the other animals. Did you notice the three planes of existence were not past, present, and future? The past did not exist except in the minds of the animals in their memories. A global memory bank of the animals' stories was saved in an online library of animalkind. The animals were not forced to work within the constraints of the old social media platforms and could create their own self-authored biography. They were encouraged annually to take time off work to self-reflect upon their year and save their memories. Whether in words, photos, videos, or art, the animals were able to write their own story and share it with the world! They could even pay a small fee to have a book printed. When a loved one passed away, their family was mailed a paperback copy of their life for their family tree.

There were so many beautiful inspiring ideas that sprang from the change of 2022, a new-age renaissance of love and thought.

Here are some of the magical words of the renegades that led the world to a bright future:

"We hold these Truths to be self-evident, that all Men are created equal, that they are endowed by their Creator with certain unalienable

Rights, that among these are Life, Liberty, and the pursuit of Happiness" (Thomas Jefferson, Declaration of Independence).

"Four score and seven years ago our fathers brought forth on this continent, a new nation, conceived in Liberty, and dedicated to the proposition that all men are created equal. . . . that we here highly resolve that these dead shall not have died in vain—that this nation, under God, shall have a new birth of freedom—and that government of the people, by the people, for the people, shall not perish from the earth" (Abraham Lincoln, "Gettysburg Address").

Virtues of Benjamin Franklin

1. TEMPERANCE. Eat not to dullness; drink not to elevation.
2. SILENCE. Speak not but what may benefit others or yourself; avoid trifling conversation.
3. ORDER. Let all your things have their places; let each part of your business have its time.
4. RESOLUTION. Resolve to perform what you ought; perform without fail what you resolve.
5. FRUGALITY. Make no expense but to do good to others or yourself; i.e., waste nothing.
6. INDUSTRY. Lose no time; be always employed in something useful; cut off all unnecessary actions.
7. SINCERITY. Use no hurtful deceit; think innocently and justly, and, if you speak, speak accordingly.
8. JUSTICE. Wrong none by doing injuries, or omitting the benefits that are your duty.
9. MODERATION. Avoid extremes; forbear resenting injuries so much as you think they deserve.
10. CLEANLINESS. Tolerate no uncleanliness in body, clothes, or habitation.
11. TRANQUILITY. Be not disturbed at trifles, or at accidents common or unavoidable.

12. CHASTITY. Rarely use venery but for health or offspring, never to dullness, weakness, or the injury of your own or another's peace or reputation.
13. HUMILITY. Imitate Jesus and Socrates.

Teachings of the Buddha

The Four Noble Truths: that suffering is an inherent part of existence; that the origin of suffering is ignorance and the main symptoms of that ignorance are attachment and craving; that attachment and craving can be ceased, and that following the Noble Eightfold Path will lead to the cessation of attachment and craving and therefore suffering.

The Noble Eightfold Path: right understanding, right thought, right speech, right action, right livelihood, right effort, right mindfulness, and right concentration.

Love. The Buddha stressed the importance of calming the mind and seeking the peace that each individual has within. With this inner peace, we can react to awkward situations with love, compassion and generosity.

> Conquer the angry man by love.
> Conquer the ill-natured man by goodness.
> Conquer the miser with generosity.
> Conquer the liar with truth. (The Dhammapada)

Power of the Mind. The Buddha taught it is our own mind which creates our own suffering, but also we can use this power to create happiness.

Your worst enemy cannot harm you as much as your own unguarded thoughts. (Lord Buddha)

All that we are is the result of what we have thought.

If a man speaks or acts with an evil thought, pain follows him.

If a man speaks or acts with a pure thought, happiness follows him, like a shadow that never leaves him. (Lord Buddha)

Jihad

Muhammad taught the concept of jihad. First and foremost, "jihad is the internal struggle against man's weaknesses such as lust, envy and hatred, and the struggle to become a better devout person. Jihad could also involve the outer battle against enemies who wished to prevent the devout from practicing their faith.

"A strong person is not the person who throws his adversaries to the ground. A strong person is the person who contains himself when he is angry" (Sunni Hadith).

The name Muhammad means "praiseworthy." Muslims he was not a divine figure but was close to a perfect man.

"And this is what Jesus means when he said: 'How is it that you can see the mote in your brother's eye and not see the beam in your own eye?' Or to put it in Moffatt's translation: 'How is it that you see the splinter in your brother's eye and fail to see the plank in your own eye?' And this is one of the tragedies of human nature. So we begin to love our enemies and love those persons that hate us whether in collective life or individual life by looking at ourselves" (Martin Luther King).

"During my lifetime I have dedicated myself to this struggle of the African people. I have fought against white domination, and I have fought against black domination. I have cherished the ideal of a democratic and free society in which all persons live together in harmony and with equal opportunities. It is an ideal which I hope to live for and to achieve. But if needs be, it is an ideal for which I am prepared to die" (Nelson Mandela, April 20, 1964).

"Whenever, O descendant of Bharata, righteousness declines and unrighteousness prevails, I manifest Myself. For the protection of the righteous and the destruction of the wicked, and for the establishment of religion, I come into being from age to age" (Sri Krishna).

"However men try to reach me, I return their love with my love; whatever path they may travel, it leads to me in the end" (Bhagavad Gita chapter 4, verse 11).

"You are only entitled to the action, never to its fruits. Do not let the fruits of action be your motive, but do not attach yourself to nonaction" (Bhagavad Gita chapter 2, verse 47).

"Sri Krishna walked the soil to annihilate the philosophies of world-shunning spirituality and of world-grasping materialism. He established on earth the 'Dharmarajya,' the Kingdom of the Inner Law. He restored the true spirit of Kshatriya heroism, motivated not by human ego, but by Divine Will, making man a devoted and active instrument of the Supreme. He brought down to the earth-consciousness the supreme Truth that earth and earthly life, being inherently divine, must be made outwardly divine, fully and totally, in every sphere, in every aspect" (Sri Chinmoy, "Commentary on the Bhagavad Gita").

"When I despair, I remember that all through history the ways of truth and love have always won. There have been tyrants, and murderers, and for a time they can seem invincible, but in the end they always fall. Think of it—always" (Gandhi).

"I am wiser than this man, for neither of us appears to know anything great and good; but he fancies he knows something, although he knows nothing; whereas I, as I do not know anything, so I do not fancy I do. In this trifling particular, then, I appear to be wiser than he, because I do not fancy I know what I do not know" (Socrates).

"In the struggle for survival, the fittest win out at the expense of their rivals because they succeed in adapting themselves best to their environment" (Charles Darwin).

"To show forbearance and gentleness in teaching others; and not to revenge unreasonable conduct—this is the energy of southern regions, and the good man makes it his study. To lie under arms; and meet death without regret—this is the energy of northern regions, and the forceful make it their study. Therefore, the superior man cultivates a friendly harmony, without being weak—How firm is he in his energy!" (Confucius, *The Doctrine of the Mean*).

"I have no more. Of all the wealth I have at my disposal, I am but the custodian for the Muslims, and I do not intend to deceive them over this and cast myself into hell-fire for your sake" (Saladin).

"Even Kings and emperors with heaps of wealth and vast dominion cannot compare with an ant filled with the love of God" (Guru Nanak, Sri Guru Granth Sahib).

Guru Nanak taught his followers three basic religious principles.

Selflessness—sharing with others, and giving to those who are less fortunate. But also selflessness of attitude—avoiding the pitfalls of egoism, pride, and jealousy.

Earning an honest living—living without deceit, exploitation, or fraud.

Naam Japna—meditating on God's name and repeating a mantra. Through the repetition of God's name, Nanak taught that a follower could free himself from selfish tendencies and cultivate happiness. However, Nanak taught it was not just enough to repeat a mantra mechanically but with selflessness and real zeal.

"There is but One God, His name is Truth, He is the Creator, He fears none, he is without hate, He never dies, He is beyond the cycle of births and death, He is self-illuminated, He is realized by the kindness of the True Guru. He was True in the beginning, He was True when the ages commenced and has ever been True, He is also True now" (Guru Nanak).

Crystal-Dawn stopped writing. It was now 9:00 p.m. The sky was darkening on another day. Hopefully she had written enough to help mankind see they had the power to do anything, and the future could be amazing if they set aside their differences to work together for the common good. It wasn't just a dream. She had worked for ten years creating a gift for all mankind, to physically see the small change they would see in their local community. There was a website that connected individuals, both local and tourist traffic to the outdoors of the region. All the outdoor activities were listed with habitat/ecosystem information, and the wildlife that lived there. Local scientific studies were shared by the main roots of the community. Businesses and organizations alike received free advertising! This gift was for the good of the people, not to be a business that earned capital by the people, for the people, which is biased and influence free. It also contained information on getting involved with volunteering in the community. The amazing people in the community, how to be a balanced, good person, everything. This website would contain the local information of the outdoor region for every region of the world. It would be connected in the same understandable format, translated into all languages. People could easily gain knowledge about an area they wished to visit and learn about the local community. They could volunteer directly with the people that needed help, saving millions of dollars donated to organizations charging good people thousands of dollars for trying to do a good deed. It should be easier for good people to do good deeds. The monies made from this book would aid in building this new online educational resource tool for communities around the world. The children of the communities would aid in writing the wildlife pages as was now the custom with huge thanks to a group of elementary students willing to write the pages for Outdoors Okanagan, making their mark on their community forever without graffiti.

Everyone wanted to be remembered for something good. This website offered a chance for communities everywhere to give back to their local community and get connected to everyone around them. The right kinds of people were made celebrities, and people strived to be remembered for their good, honorable actions.

The first time this dream was presented to three MLA government officials, Crystal-Dawn held a scrapbook containing pages she had made to show what the website would look like. She gained one support letter. She was then visibly missing her eye tooth and half her teeth in the back. She must have looked like quite the prole at that time. It was now seven years later, and Crystal had since lost all her teeth but was still kicking. The website was developed as much as she could to show the world what was required, and it would take the world's best programmers to build it, not her. If the MLAs had helped Crystal back then, not only could they have saved her personally from the pitfalls of a prole, but this website would also have been live during the great Covid. The people of the communities would have had a way to connect and try a variety of outdoor activities. The entire world and even a generation of children felt the effects of disconnectedness. Some still choose to wear a mask to hide their beautiful faces. People have always been insecure about their appearance, and these masks became a free pass to hide from the world.

She wanted to be a crystal dawn for all the people to see the world for what it truly was, a beautiful, loving, rainbow of light.

> Frère Jacques
> Frère Jacques
> Dormez vous?
> Dormez vous?
> Sonnez les matines
> Sonnez les matines
> Ding, ding, dong
> Ding, ding, dong

www.outdoorsokanagan.ca

May 14, 2022

You thought it was over, didn't you? Of course not! "This is the song that never ends. Yes, it goes on and on, my friends. Some people started singing it, not knowing what it was, and they'll continue singing it forever just because this is the song that never ends."

It was the weekend again, so they traveled to Kelowna for their youngest daughter's gymnastics competition. She did great and was so surrounded by loved ones! They had a great day and stopped at the cemetery so Gerrasimos could meet Andy. It was rather special for Crystal to have the two special men in her life meeting. He also saw the Grist Mill and its story lived again through Crystal's tales. She gathered some sage and spent the evening wrapping smudge sticks.

A lot had occurred over the last two weeks, yet it was just a speck of living in the full accumulation of one's lifetime. There was so much more to come. This truly was just the beginning.

Bhakti is an intense love and devotion for God, life, energy, and creation. While some may strive for it in their lives, there are others that are plagued by it. With great love comes great disappointment. One had to thoroughly study the difference between hope and expectation to be able to determine where the pain could be avoided. You see Crystal loved Gerrasimos so greatly that it did not matter if he existed on another plane and did not return her exact emotions. Sometimes she felt the sting of perceived rejection, and it caused an issue, but for the most part, she always recognized it and never thought less of Gerrasimos, only herself. For surely, she had not yet proven herself worthy of the love she sought. She would aspire to try harder. His solution was to shut people out, which only demonstrated how much he needed to see her example.

Hello Lover,

You think you messed up our date but you did not. Despite having a conversation about not liking the sharing of feelings, you shared your feelings, which is never a bad thing. In fact it is a good thing and I appreciate you opening the door to your soul that helps me understand you a little better.

I consider you to be wise. Sometimes I seek your suggestions. Sometimes you have some. Sometimes you don't. Both are okay. You're not expected to have all the answers. You get lost in rambling about engines and cars and wood, and I in, well, perhaps you'd be the one to answer that one best in the activities of others? Perhaps when worded that way, it suggests perhaps I should just keep to my own business and focus on myself and less on the activities of others. So if I have hit the nail here let me know 'cause I think perhaps it's not the talking about of feelings, but it's the feelings in regard to the actions and activities of others or perhaps just anything negative in general? This is where I get a little stumped and think about it. What is it I need to not do? I do believe I'm the one to blame for ruining a date if anybody. I still always enjoy time with you and the opportunity to help someone. That felt good. I haven't tagged along on helping excursions lately, lacking the helping feeling, but that was good, so good.

Highlights . . . you are an amazing person.
I love the fuck out of you.
I know you're capable of amazing big things, and I'm going to help you do it.

You are a light in the darkness.
You're a sudden cool breeze on a stifling day.

You're a joyful loving thought, a solid riverbank that contains my wild river yet allows it to flow freely.

Your soul has depths to which I am not currently trained or equipped to dive, but if you teach me, I'd like to stay there forever.

He would ask her why did the world matter so much. Why did the security and well-being of their own family not come first?

Crystal-Dawn recognized the importance of helping the world. Everyone, everyone was in pain. Everybody needed love and hope. Without it, their children's future would be filled with even more pain. She could not send her children out into an uncaring world. Neither could she shield them all from it. The world needed to change. They wanted the change. Everyone wants love. Everyone wants to be heard and respected. Everyone wants to live a full, joyful life, surrounded by delicious, healthy food, friendly fluffy animals, and loving family and friends. It was possible if they worked together with this common goal for mankind.

God used to be Crystal's best friend, not since birth but since she was ten years old and thrown off a cliff, twice, by "bad association". She shut out the world and drew close to her father. She was baptized at twelve in the same city she now resides. She wanted to be like Hannah. Hannah was listed in the Old Testament as being one of God's friends. She was never found away from the temple. Crystal used to walk to the kingdom hall on lunch breaks to sit on the front steps and read the Bible. She even skipped classes to sit there sometimes. She couldn't go in as Jehovah's Witnesses keep their doors locked when not in service. Soon they put in a gate as well. She drew strength singing his praises in the sunshine, even if it was outside the gate on the rocky ground. He knew she needed it. When she returned to school, she would enter the classroom and one boy would shout, "When I say weak ass, y'all say bitch, weak ass." And then a chorus of voices would call, "Bitch." Again, he would rally, "Weak ass," and they would return his call, "Bitch." A final third call resounded through the classroom, "Weak ass" followed by a final triumphant, "Bitch!"

That was high school. Then 9/11 occurred that fall. It opened a door to a prole to escape her community and see the world for what it truly was. How else could a prole have afforded a flight internationally if not for a tragedy to make flights affordable? Her father never forgave her for that. The London shoe bomb occurred while she was in England. That was all the evidence he needed the world was unsafe. Crystal-Dawn refused to believe the world was a bad place. One day she would join President Putin on a hunting trip, and they would discuss the people of Russia. She would help heal his soul and open his eyes to the plight of the people. She would stand before the United Nations and say, "This is the day we declare peace and security. We the people thank you for your service thus far, but we'll take the reins from here. All of us with the proper guidance from the individuals who give their lives studying our world to make it a better place for all of us."

She stopped being a Jehovah's Witness at nineteen because she wanted to connect with the people around her. She had to reason if she was willing to break God's law, that must mean that she did not believe in his existence because she could not do such things if she believed in him. Have you ever watched movies where strong Catholics are beating themselves, scars lining their backsides? Many would never understand why someone would do such a thing, but Crystal knew. When she prayed, her prayers went like this:

> Dear Jehovah God, our Father in the heavens,
> Thank you so much for this beautiful day you have bestowed upon us!
> Thank you for the food that fills our plates, and the loving friends and family in my life.

You see Crystal had no problem being official to begin with. She was after all addressing the Supreme Being of the universe, her creator. There were formalities to such affairs.

But God was also her best friend. He was the one that was always there by her side, so she wasn't alone. Surely their conversations were not always formal. The problem occurred when Crystal would suddenly realize she didn't know how much time had passed since she began praying, but in her thoughts of her family and friends and the day's events, she had stumbled upon "inappropriate thoughts". For surely you were not supposed to be thinking of a boy at school having a cute butt when in the audience of the greatest Supreme Being. She had been sitting at the feet of the court of the Almighty and all His angels sharing thoughts of a boy's cute butt.

That was not okay.

She would feel so terribly dreadful for this offense as she was an imperfect human. She begged forgiveness and cried and sobbed. If she had just concluded the prayer with, "Through your Son Christ Jesus, amen." It would have been okay. Her mind could have wandered anywhere if she had just concluded her audience with the Almighty by acknowledging his Son's sacrifice to open this channel of communication. She did not and therefore was a terrible friend. She did not have Bhakti for God, it was concluded.

If Crystal was with Gerrasimos, she would never do such a thing. If they were speaking, she would not simply wander off in thought and forget that they had been in conversation. She would not purposefully or knowingly do anything that would cause him pain or problems. She knew she was to be his healing oasis. That was Bhakti. She had Bhakti for people.

George Orwell teaches us that we need to connect and love each other because as soon as we give up on one another, the machine has won. Have great Bhakti for all. It will heal the Earth.

She began composing a psalm for Gerrasimos.

1. Oh, Lover of mine, how I long for your embrace! Your incredible body fills me with such delight! The sight of you, your smell, your touch, I crave and feel throughout my entire being. Our minds can dance as one in an intricate yet free flow of enjoyment.
2. Every moment used to its Greatest Purpose and Joy possible is one spent with you. A Best Friend of amazing intellect and

kindness. His Third Eye is open to all yet directs no attention to himself.

3. Oh, Great One, if you could but see yourself through the eyes of your Lover. You would see your immense strength is like that of a Mountain. You would see the Undiscovered Depths of your Soul. The most entrancing of Siren Songs calls deep from Within. It escapes as but a whistle. A harmonious whistle of familiarity. Whether Old or New, your Song touches my Soul and gravitates me to you.

4. How men do not quake before you is evidenced by way of your warm smile. There is no Badness within you. No ill will or injustice of any sort. You are the Most Loving Father, imparting your wisdom to any that will hear.

5. Your Smile reveals a Joyful Recognition and playful Innocence like that of a Childhood Friend.

6. How many hills we have rolled down, I do not know. What is known is that you have been in my Thoughts, Always.
Since the Dawn of Time, I have carried you with me,
Deep in my Soul. Protected and Entrusted to a Power
far beyond that of my Heart. To the Universe, to All.

7. My Love for you is so Great it exceeds Myself, that Others should know of your Greatness and Love you too.

8. How could one so amazing not be Loved and Appreciated by All.
And when one day I fall and my earthly body no longer sustains the consciousness that is me within, I will have ensured you are surrounded by Love.

9. I will still fill your mind with beautiful thoughts of Hope, Love, and Joy.
You will not weep my loss because in my lifetime you gave me the Greatest Gift of All—Your Love.

10. It was with that Love I was able to be joyful and see the World for the Beautiful Place it was because you were in it.
Surely a World that Created You cannot be Bad. It must be a World of Beauty and Love.

I was able to live countless days of my life feeling your loving embrace, and that is what makes Life worth Living.
Loving and being Loved.
11. You're not Perfect. None of us are. But you're Perfect for me, and I shall strive to be perfect for you. Bhakti.

One Final Resurrection—Ronald

Ronald was a young boy in Calgary. Perhaps around the age of seven, he lived in a townhouse complex in the NE. He was your typical fun-loving boy of the late eighties and early nineties that played outdoors in the neighborhood and built forts. One day, he and his friends discovered a space between a wooden retaining wall and the earth bank. It was the perfect area to hang out and build a fort. Children love building. They gathered supplies and created the ultimate hangout area for a kid their age. Crystal-Dawn had a brother the same age as these boys. He wasn't allowed to play in the fort because those kids were not of the same faith. Crystal herself had already had her mouth washed out with soap for asking what fuck meant and an ass whooping for inspiring all the neighborhood kids to slide down the windshield of her mom's new Firenza. They weren't allowed to play with those kids very often.

The fort was amazing though for the kids that were allowed in. Crystal never got to see it herself but heard tales of blankets, crazy carpets, and candles.

That was how the fire started, started with candles, fueled by blankets and crazy carpets.

The firemen couldn't remove the wooden boards of the retaining walls in time. A mother lost her son that day. It was possible more children perished, but it was Ronald that was burned into Crystal's memory. Her mother had offered Ronald's mother a tract as typical of a Jehovah's Witness to help aid a grieving one with their loss with hope for a new world, a resurrection. The lesson we can learn and remember is this. Ronald spent a lot of his time and energy and resources making a nice place for himself and his friends. It ended up being their death trap. Just because we have spent a lot of effort working on our current society, it does not mean it is good for us. In fact it is a death trap, and there are a lot of innocent people depending on us to make the change needed.

> Follow the Moskva, down to Gorky Park, listening to the wind of change.
>
> An August summer night, soldiers passing by, listening to the wind of change.
>
> The world is closing in, did you ever think that we could be so close, like brothers?
>
> The future's in the air, can feel it everywhere, blowing with the wind of change.
>
> Take me to the magic of the moment, on a glory night, where the children of tomorrow dream away in the wind of change.
>
> Walking down the street, distant memories are buried in the past, forever.
>
> The wind of change blows straight into the face of time, like a storm wind that will ring the freedom bell for peace of mind.
>
> (Scorpions, "Wind of Change")